The University As Text

The University As Text
Women and the University Context

Carol Schick

Fernwood Publishing
Halifax

Editing: Anne Webb
Cover design: Dan Coggins
Design and production: Beverley Rach
Printed and bound in Canada by Hignall Printing Limited.

A publication of

Fernwood Publishing
Box 9409 Station A
Halifax, Nova Scotia
B3K 5S3

Canadian Cataloguing in Publication Data

Schick, Carol.

The university as text

Includes bibliographical references.
ISBN 1-895686-33-4

1. Women--Education (Higher) 2. Sexism in education. 3. Feminism and education. I. Title.

LC1567.S34 1994 370.19'345 C94-950079-8

Contents

Acknowledgements

Many people assisted me in the accomplishment of this book, and none more than my friends who shared space with me in the graduate students' study room. I am sure I learned from the conversations, questions, and enthusiasm offered by each person; their encouragement never ceased to surprise and sustain me.

I especially acknowledge the untiring work of Dr. Irene Poelzer, Professor Emerita, at the University of Saskatchewan. I count myself among the many people who have been inspired by her commitment to improving feminist pedagogy and scholarship for the benefit of all. I also wish to thank other advisors turned friends: Michael Collins and Adrian Blunt.

It has been a pleasure to work with the people involved in the book's production at Fernwood Publishing. Their commitment and integrity in publishing books that work toward social change is commendable. The insightful and careful work of Beverley Rach, Anne Webb, and Errol Sharpe have been especially significant in accomplishing this book.

I owe a debt of gratitude to my family and friends Dan Coggins, Alma Schick, Charles Schick, and Margaret Dutli for their gifts of love and support. For their encouragement in times past and in the present, I express my love and thanks.

Preamble

When I returned to university as a mature student, after many years of teaching in Canadian public schools, I observed that, among undergraduate students at least, few things had changed. Accomplishing a degree still required that students separate their knowledge and desires from the seemingly unattainable, distant knowledge of figures of authority. What passed for education was often an individualizing, objectifying process. Students adapted well and usually managed to resist the most enthusiastic offer to become personally involved in the content of the class, the content never being more important to the students than the project of learning the the essence of the university itself. This experience was common to many students.

I later identified some of the fallout of this cynical process in my own life when I found it increasingly difficult to choose a thesis topic to research and write about. I did not know or was unaccustomed to naming where my real interests lay. The process of asserting my own personal choice in the context of so much external authority was an overwhelming task. I seemed completely incapable of naming any but the most superficial of interests.

One particular experience in a seminar class crystallized my observations about the nature of learning at the university. While working on a topic that did interest me a great deal, I realized that my reading, interpreting, and speaking were all externally controlled experiences. I saw very clearly how public, male-generated, Eurocentric knowledge came to represent the total of what was worth knowing at the university and of how we could think about it. I understood that I could research anything I wanted and that my work would be taken seriously as long as my interpretation and analysis fell within the bounds of Eurocentric, male thought. Any other interpretation was on its own and would be evaluated according to the values of the hegemonic knowledge.

As research topics flooded into my mind, I saw that the university's definition of knowledge was not just racist or sexist, but ensured that marginalized voices could not speak in anything but previously defined roles. We cannot interpret the world in ways that represent our experiences if the criteria for what is worth knowing has already been set for us. Furthermore, if our interpretations and representations are categorically defined as unacceptable and other, then our otherness is also unacceptable.

In the following chapters, which initially formed a thesis, I discuss the difficulty of representing women as women in the university context given the organization of knowledge and structure found there. Locating academic discourse strictly in the abstract, the impersonal, and the male-defined leaves a gap between academic discourse—where many people including women and people of colour are objects—and the place where women, people of colour, and other marginalized groups represent themselves as subjects. Being in the gap of non-representation is a scary, disempowering experience; writing one's way out of it is to proclaim the truth.

My perspective is informed by writings of and conversations with others, but my interpretation of the university context is grounded in my own experience. I am reclaiming my narrative voice as authoritative, but I contine to wonder to what extent my narrative is valuable both to the reader/listener and to me. Describing personal experience can be cathartic; in the feminist classroom, it also needs to be revelatory. Meaning is created in the background and present context of one's narrative and, in hearing the narratives of others, we are awakened to a knowledge of our own experience.

Writing my thesis was a profoundly frightening experience because I was exposing myself to both criticism of my research and to rejection of my subjective self. I was not blithely telling what happened to me, and I recognized that women's public participation in the life of the university can promote violence on many levels. When I defended this work as a thesis, I invited many supporters to attend what is usually a small event attended by five or six people. In spite of a wonderfully supportive thesis committee, I wanted witnesses to observe the outcome of a thesis defence that criticized the hegemonic knowledge found at the university. I also wanted to use the supporters' collective courage.

People often try to disguise the fact that their book began as a thesis. Clearly, I have not tried to do this; thesis writing is an important artifact and representation of university knowledge.

Chapter 1 introduces the problem of interpreting the university context from an anti-racist, anti-sexist perspective that is generally seen as peripheral to the university project. In Chapter 2 I discuss the feminist interpretation I engage and provide an overview of the university context, its assumptions about research, and its disciplinary approach to knowledge. I identify some of the barriers to women's incorporation of their experience and knowledge as women into the university, such as the overdetermined structures that reflect Eurocentric, men's experience.

The third chapter features a feminist interpretation in a specific discipline, English literature. An historical examination of the university's literary canon reveals its domination by men's interests and aesthetics, and its erasure of women's interests, unstereotypical women characters, and women's work as producers of characters in literature. A feminist interpretation of texts challenges those interpretive theories that either ignore or objectify women and people of colour, but claim to be apolitical. The feminist literary theory which abandons a definition of "essential woman" must then come to terms with women's representation as subjects.

The final chapter in some ways begins the real work. Here I discuss the process of feminist pedagogy. This process is contrary to the organizational, methodological, disciplinary, and philosophical approaches of traditional university activities. In attempting to apply feminist pedagogical practices, the administration, students, and even professors committed to the issues do not find it easy to envisage practices that have few precedents and may, indeed, contradict notions of what was formerly thought to be important. I demonstrate that practising feminist pedagogy—based on life experiences and feminist theory—in the university essentially entails practising in an anathematic milieu.

In this work I interpret the university context in a way that resists closure and definition, not from contrariness on my part, but because I view knowledge as an event, not a localized commodity. As an event, knowledge never ceases to change and unfold with time, as the following example illustrates.

Since completing this work as a thesis, I have learned many things about racial oppression that would have made the outcome of this writing look quite different if it were possible to go back and live the same moment twice. My present, on-going understanding of racial oppression is something I did not possess on first writing this study. I am aware, however, that even though the study does not deal in any substantive way with the issue of race, it would be impossible to try to pretend that it did by imposing words about racism over top of this existing text and subtext which is essentially about gender. I acknowledge that a study about the university context in which I have privileged gender oppression is limited without a thorough-going analysis of race. I recommend the study of race as a direction for continued writing and research.

The hermeneutic approach I have chosen draws on both public and private knowledge and experience. In view of knowledge being socially constructed and partial, I have not assumed to define knowledge in the university context, but have prepared an interpretive event in which you are invited to participate.

CHAPTER ONE

The Context for Reading and Writing

The Western, middle-class, male hegemony over the creation of knowledge at universities is being called into question, often by those who are not Western, middle-class, or male. Wanting more than minimal participation in the university, those who are not part of its original elite are challenging several traditional notions, including what counts as knowledge, how knowledge may be recognized, and whose version of knowledge is credible. The masculinist patterns of university life that define issues, disciplines, practices, life expectations, and social interactions situate women and many men on the periphery of the institution. A feminist interpretation of the university context is needed to reveal and provide alternatives to these traditional patriarchal patterns which exclude "outsiders."

The masculinist interpretation of knowledge and practice at the university has so successfully projected its own ways of seeing social reality "that its view is accepted as common sense and as part of the natural order" (Jagger 1983, as cited in Lewis 1990,151). This hegemony is what makes a feminist interpretation both difficult to accomplish and necessary. In particular, feminist pedagogy, as a practical application of feminist theory, raises problems requiring solutions which are beyond the scope of traditional understandings of pedagogy. This book thus undertakes a feminist interpretation of the university in spite of the exclusion and marginalization of women's experience and knowledge.

I focus primarily on reading and the interpretation of texts we encounter throughout our lives. Literary texts that exemplify interpretation in a formal sense are but one facet of our ongoing process of reading and understanding. This study questions the efficacy of one interpretation over others and suggests that the history of undervaluing interpretations made by marginalized groups has left all readers poorer. The limitations imposed by patriarchal practices at the university affect "the health and strength of our universities as a centre of scholarly research and teaching" (Smith 1991, 1). Teaching feminist theory and practice at the university not only adds to the stock of knowledge; it affirms that all people have the right to define the world from their own experience. What is problematic is the hostile environment facing such teaching.

My commitment to this study comes from my experience of anomalies in the public and private representation of women. I have observed, as have many others, that even when women have the same knowledge and perform the same jobs as men, women are discounted as women. Clearly the power differential of men over women depends on more than women's ability to perform men's public roles. In the pages that follow, I discuss not only the categorization of knowledge, but the use of gender as a criterion on which to evaluate and interpret knowledge.

I have also noted that in public, women's private knowledge is considered of little value. For example, women's private diaries and journals have, until recently, been disregarded as sources of information about women; even still that knowledge is often seen to be of questionable worth. As a way of exemplifying the relevance of this personal form, I begin each of the following chapters with a journal entry in which I consider my own experience of the university.

In "Toward a Women-Centered University," Adrienne Rich (1979) acknowledges that while the title of her essay may sound far-fetched, it helps us realize that the opposite—a men-centred university—is, in fact, what now exists. As a male-dominated institution, the university tradition and the male tradition are one. Facts and research methods are generated and taught according to a male intellectual tradition. Although some may argue that women are not outside but inside the university system, it is important to recognize that women's work is valued differently. The dearth of women in tenured positions, the paucity of women's names on publications and reading lists, their infrequent involvement in decision making, and the invisibility of work done by women at all levels of the hierarchy confirm that women are, at best, silent insiders.

Rich asks some important questions about the nature of learning at the university. She wonders whether the means of changing society can be learned in a setting that is already over-determined in its structure, thoroughly sedimented in its practices, and not particularly interested in significant change. She suggests that, for women, there is a great deal at stake when it comes to questioning the existing tradition—and even more at stake for leaving the tradition as it is.

Women's integrity in a university setting is compromised in terms of both the content they teach and the hierarchical structure they teach in. The content in most disciplines obscures women's experience by assuming either that male experiences speak for all or that women's experiences are universally alike. In many cases research about women has either not been done at all, or has been added as a footnote to the existing body of knowledge. Margrit Eichler (1988) has noted several ways in which so-called "objective" research methodologies have subsumed facts about women. As a result women students generally find little which reflects the world as they see it, and many come to accept the "facts" as they are presented. Anne Walsh suggests that for women students, "the absence of women writers in university literary curricula together with the minority of women teachers contributes to a material, intellectual and psychic deprivation" (1986, 8).

That is not to say that male students do not also find the university experience alien at times. The objectification of both "truth" and the student body seems unhealthy for all. For some males, however, the alienation arises from women no longer being so eager, as Virginia Woolf (1982 [1929]) suggests, to hold up a mirror which reflects men's images at twice their natural size (1982, 35). Women are concerned instead, with finding or establishing reflections of their own experiences in the knowledge and traditions of academia.

Critiquing the University from the Inside

As mentioned in the preamble, this book began its life as a thesis. Some reference to its former status is important to include, particularly given that it demonstrates that a student may formally criticize the institution granting his or her degree. While the search for knowledge at a university can surely withstand critique, does the acceptance of a critical thesis in fact contradict this book's argument—that women's interests are suppressed in the university? Perhaps the acceptance of a critical thesis is not the issue; the content may be considered secondary as long as the traditional rules of presentation have been followed. I would suggest that tradition and the structure of knowledge have grown like ivy around the university, secluding it from knowledge that contradicts the existing paradigm, especially knowledge about women.

A thesis criticizing the university is no threat at all, even when it is the traditional values, methods, and structures that a discussion of women's issues takes exception to. The university tradition may, by virtue of its respect for academic freedom, permit and even invite criticism and discussion on feminist theory as proof that the university is an open institution where debate is alive and well. It is quite another matter, however, to have feminist demands acted upon on university campuses.

Indeed, university communities often respond begrudgingly, and sometimes with violence, to feminist critiques that ask for real institutional change.

Feminists' participation in the university is one method among many to resist the continuation of patriarchal domination in that feminist theory making and practice contribute to social change and to the very notion that change is possible. Feminist knowledge challenges the university's elitist way of viewing the world. If a feminist perspective is absent, what the university reproduces is a systemically distorted notion of knowledge that is inadequate for both female and male students, and for meeting the challenges of justice and equality being contested daily in society.

That the university is an elitist institution is not news to anyone. The traditional university education was designed for and by upper- and middle-class white men. The fact that well over half the undergraduate population nowadays is made up of people who are neither middle-class, white, nor male has resulted in little change. The generation and teaching of facts, as well as the research, continues to be accomplished according to a male intellectual tradition. In spite of the university tradition which claims to see knowledge as open to debate, testing, and proof, those who are university educated are likely to judge their education as good, and unlikely to take seriously critical remarks that come from outside the university walls (Grant 1969, 31).

Critique of the university from a feminist perspective encompasses more than an examination of gender equity or studies of how female students and faculty can interact more successfully with the university system. A feminist critique of the university examines its structures, that is the bureaucracies, hierarchies, and traditions that entrench practice by the sheer weight of their persistence. The criteria for judging the university structure as inadequate arises most readily from positions that are marginal to or outside the university tradition; of course, those within the university system tend to believe that criticism from outside need not be taken seriously. I suggest that a feminist critique which takes seriously issues of race and class, and is accompanied by the proposal of a feminist pedagogy, is a sound criterion which comes from such a marginal position.

The Basis of the Argument

This work is supported by historical and current feminist scholarship that challenges the tradition of the university as a context in which the representation of women is marginalized. I have tried to problematize the categories of thinking that objectify knowledge and place limits on what counts as evidence; in this regard, the orientation of this work clearly runs counter to the positivistic research tradition. Feminist scholarship is more than information about women, it is also a way of thinking which resists the separation of knowledge from experience. I have adopted a hermeneutical approach in my writing that both interprets and demonstrates that knowledge is partial, not fixed, and always in process. In reading the book you will see that, insofar as I am able, I have avoided a linear, empirical structuring of knowledge in favour of one that is deconstructive, interpretive, and personal.

My research has been guided by my understanding of poststructuralism as it intersects with feminist philosophy. The works of Chris Weedon, Linda Nicholson, Jonathan Culler, and Michel Foucault have been particularly instructive, as has the writing of feminist literary critics Elaine Showalter, Joanne Frye, and Mary Jacobus.

Two extended metaphors that I use throughout the book are the act of reading and the interpretation of texts. The everyday events of the university tradition are compared to a text which can be read and interpreted for its meaning. As one would read in the literal sense, I "read" the university (con)text to see what meaning I can take from it, especially regarding the position of women.

I have described my activity in this book by saying that I am going to "critique" the university structure, and "look at" the context in which this critique takes place. The purpose is not only to critique, but also to elucidate some of the assumptions about procedures and events at the university which discriminate against women and which are called normal. Examining "norms" is important because they provide a backdrop against which women's positionality, representation, and voice are carried out. More than a critique, however, this work asserts the right of women to assume central positions in their own understanding and interpretation of this academic context. That women have the right to interpret contexts from their points of view as women is founded in the same justice claim that is used by women to negotiate concrete issues of equitable wages or representation on course reading lists. The struggle is not just with the conditions or effects of patriarchal structures, but with the influence of these contexts on women's reading and the interpretation of their own lives.

Methodology as Matrix

Determining what is the appropriate methodology to use is a major issue in feminist research as the methodological structuring of a problem presupposes what kind of knowledge may be included in the answer. The issue of methodology, therefore, is most germane to this work. In the writing process, the issue of methodology has been, for me, the most difficult part.

Although there is no single model of feminist methodology, all feminist research takes seriously the notion that the method must fit the problem and not the reverse. For feminists, the method becomes part of the problem: as we mediate the problem through the chosen methodology, we are constantly checking our language and perceptions to see which voice and whose words are being used. We are always checking to see what has been omitted and what difference it makes in a way that Dorothy Smith describes as "making the everyday problematic." As women, we are in the midst of articulating our values as we establish and put them into practice, so that to say is also to do; and knowledge is constructed and reconstructed as a process. To speak of methodology is not simply a formality or a preliminary exercise that takes place before we get to the interpretive data. In the methodology, the interpretation has already begun.

The methodology used for this study is centred on the compilation and interpretation of feminist writing in the areas of literature, education, and philosophy. Much writing has been done on the topic of women's experience as both teachers and students in academic institutions. Some writers draw on personal experience in the university and combine their reflection on their experience with their knowledge of particular subjects—such as literature, education, philosophy—to report and theorize about women's issues.

A second major body of literature directly relevant to this study is that of literary criticism and theories of interpretation. I have chosen a critical feminist point of view without debating its efficacy or responding to literary criticism that ignores gender issues and thereby reinforces the male hegemony over the interpretation of texts. Supporting texts are chosen for the aptness of their contribution to the production and reproduction of women's interpreting voices.

There is no single author whose work I have referred to more consistently than any others. The teaching experiences, philosophical discussions, and theorizing of different writers indicate a wide range of questions and points of view. What emerges when these various sources are compared is not quite a pattern but a chimera of patterns, most noticeable at the point of their dissolution. The diverging and converging patterns imply that knowledge is not so much a thing to be grasped as it is a way of momentarily understanding the connectedness and revelation of ideas. Such patterns are also found in feminist pedagogy which is not prescriptive and immutable, but personal, reflective, and emergent.

What follows is a discussion of some of the assumptions I have made in writing this book that have become almost invisible to me due to their familiarity. It is always difficult to know what needs to be rendered visible as only with difficulty can we think as outsiders about many of our assumptions. Consequently, the issues I clarify are not necessarily the most important ones, but rather the ones that are easiest for me to notice. The assumptions that I do not mention may in some ways be more germane to what I am writing, but it is their very embeddedness that makes them less accessible and, consequently, unrevealed.

The first assumption is that the Western male experience is not universal and neither is any other. Second, since one's gender affects a person's interpretation, and since men and women are differently situated in the social structure, their readings will be different. Third, in that reading as a woman is possible, it is this reading which is emphasized in this text. Last, my interpretation is an expression of my experience, my research, my ideology, my effective history, and the way in which I am socially constructed.

Because I am talking about "reading" the university while positioned inside it, my source of information is all around me. I have chosen to base much of my research on the reading of books, journals, and articles found in the library and in private collections. Other sources were available to me and would have resulted in an equally fruitful and perhaps quite different reading. For example, I could have set out to gather information from sitting in on classes, systematically interviewing students and teachers, observing interactions in various departments, or documenting many other instances of women's encounters with the university. In some ways, all of these activities have been an informal part of my reading as I have, at some time or other, engaged in all of them. The encouragement and criticism of friends and acquaintances have also contributed to my reading process, as have the numerous conversations, intense debates, news about others' research, and "must read" articles pressed on me by others.

Now, as I interpret the meaning of what I have read, I see even more clearly that by virtue of my positioning I am simultaneously the researcher and part of the researched. The possibilities for reading are wide open; however, my criterion for interpretation—to read as a woman—is not. What is open, and resists closure, is the definition of what a woman might be, in this text or in any other. Mary Jacobus (1986) and many other feminist literary critics contest the representation of women in texts, especially those texts whose form is already overdetermined by masculinist codes. That academic writing is thoroughly male encoded makes this question of representation pertinent to the methodology of this book.

Are there women's ways of doing thesis writing and presenting research at the university, where it is assumed that the male model is universal and gender is not an issue? Similar questions of how the feminine emerges are the topic of Mary Jacobus's (1986) chapter "Is There a Woman in This Text?" Jacobus's answer for the particular text she is describing is equivocal. My response is likewise qualified: yes, there is a woman in this text in that I have recorded my own experience and observations as those of a woman; yet no, in that I as the speaking subject am immersed in the masculine tradition; yet, perhaps yes again as even though I have been encoded in the masculinist tradition, I have foregrounded my feminist point of view. This question of the representation of women in texts and contexts is important and one which I invite you to consider as you read. The issue of women's ways of doing thesis writing and other academic activities is whether, and how, they can be present as women, or whether they will always be offering a female version of men's work. An important project of this book is to investigate how we may overcome the latter by discovering the former.

Academic Style

The academic style of writing requires that a person perform a ventriloquist-like act of separating her sentient body from her speaking voice. Academic writing regards the influence of the personal as an unreliable source of knowledge. The assumption is that works which are capable of revealing great knowledge and authority are both objective and disembodied. When I first wrote this work as a thesis, using the personal voice was, and in some quarters still is, a questionable practice. As I could not conceive of the work in any other way, I proceeded in the first person singular. Beginning from my own experience, I was better able to illustrate with integrity the notion that knowledge is socially constructed and that the personal and the intellectual are not opposing qualities.

That is not to say that feminist writing is merely confessional, simplistic, or even easy. One of the most difficult things to do when writing, particularly in academic settings, is include the personal; I have had to struggle against my own inclination to objectify my experience and to remove myself to the outside. Formal acceptance of my first person perspective has not released me from long-standing habits of academic writing in which theory is more credible than experiences, as is abstraction rather than the concrete, and speculation of the "other" rather than the subjective "I." To remain personal, to own what I am saying, and to stay in the centre of this discourse takes all my courage and honesty when what I really want to do is flee to the sidelines to postulate *about* what I have learned, a process that would leave me safe and the learning opaque. But, while the act of reflection enables me to answer the question, "What does this mean?" I also want to be able to answer, "What does this mean to me?" What I am learning is to stay in the middle, to read, to engage, and to be a person, one who can see that you are a person too.

Writing as a woman from the centre of my knowing is not easy to do, partly because other kinds of writing are so ingrained, and partly because of the risk of personal revelation. I suggest that as we continue to reveal our own experience as evidence, we will expand the parameters for academic writing as a form of praxis.

The University Context

The structure that serves to keep people, ideas, and disciplines apart at the university is epitomized by the hierarchical order, the style of discourse, the depersonalization, the use of power and technology as ends rather than means, and confusion between human beings and objects. The effect is distancing—it keeps one in one's place, and contains challenges so that only those which fall within the guidelines, that is, within the disciplinary paradigm can be launched. These abstract regulators and other impediments affect both women and men who attend the university, but insofar as a masculine culture prevails, women succeed only to the extent they can become "amateur males" (Rich 1979, 134).

The dehumanizing effect of the university system of education is addressed by both feminist and adult education theory. Paulo Freire's (1974) banking concept of education is typified at the university level, where liberatory learning is given up in exchange for the highest level of academic certification. Feminist theory insists that attention be paid to the social and material conditions of women's lives, especially when the conditions affect what and how students learn. Feminist theory takes issue with "well-meaning" programs that do superficial work to address women's issues but do not address the limited approaches to knowledge production found at the university.

As this study is a critique of university structures and activities, it is the type of criticism that Jonathan Culler regards as a "breeding ground for facile polemic" (1988, viii). He suggests that radical criticism levelled against institutions generally assumes that the inherent force of themes such as racism, sexism, and imperialism would be released to pursue their political ends if they could by-pass the institutional structures that order and contain them. The way in which institutional structures domesticate radical discourse is a favourite theme of criticism and results in a diatribe that exposes the fault of one system, while advocating the reforms of the latest discourse. It is the desire to find another method to bring about these efficacious, political acts that produces "an interest in the institutional and ideological dimensions of criticism itself" (Culler 1988, xiii).

As a large social institution, the university is not infrequently the target of public criticism and it takes no special ability to offer a critique of its organization and structure. In spite of Culler's scepticism of yet another critique that comes to dominate other lines of thought, his words about the nature of structures are worth noting. He suggests that the university is not simply a monolithic enterprise set in place by malevolent designs against women, racial minorities, and the poor. Beyond the physical structures, course outlines, rules and regulations, the university context is also a forum in which processes are changing patterns.

The context of the university is more than a place where things happen; the context also affects and includes what happens. The interpretation of a context requires the elucidation and interpretation of the events that produce the context. When I speak of the university context, I mean its determined structures and processes that set the university in motion, as well as the fluctuating assumptions about how the processes should be carried out. As the processes have socially constituted interpretations, and meanings, I use this study to look at some of the values, institutional arrangements, and practices that become known collectively as the university context.

The Centrality of Reading

A metaphor that I find convenient for this examination of the university is that of reading a text. Just as we read and interpret texts, we are constantly interpreting and taking meaning from our surroundings. Like the words, sentences, or paragraphs of a text, human action is an event that is open to a range of interpretations and references which decide its meaning. As we take meaning from texts, so we take meanings from the events that occur around us. Paul Ricoeur says that "all significant events and deeds are . . . opened to this kind of practical interpretation through present *praxis*. Human action, too, is opened to anybody who *can read*" (Ricoeur, 1981, 208).

Just as a text is open to the interpretation of those who read it, the context for human activity—such as the university—is open to interpretation. This idea of reading the university as text is not only a metaphor; reading in order to interpret is what goes on any time someone interacts or encounters the university context. Insofar as one is more or less involved with the university, one cannot stop interpreting it. A constant reading, interpreting, and understanding in order to decide what to do next is a requirement of functioning within any context.

This study looks at reading in both a literal sense and in a metaphorical sense. When I address feminist pedagogy in the teaching of English literature, reading is a literal event. But the ongoing metaphor of context as text slips easily between figurative and literal applications. For example, in this study, I simply read literally and figuratively what I see around me at the university; to narrow the topic, I choose part of the context to read; and in the act of reading I begin what I think is the most problematic aspect of all—how I will read. By this I mean that the point of view I may use, and experiences and prejudices I bring to the reading event cannot be separated from my interpretation in this study. The fact that my reading is coloured by these variables is not, in itself, unusual. The location of the reader within a context is not only commonplace, it could not be otherwise. The reader is always situated in some context that presupposes what and how she or he will perceive and understand. The problem of reading the university is deciding who may read, what may be read, and whose reading will be aloud. It is not simply a matter of getting permission or being allowed to speak. In the case of a feminist interpretation, one wonders whether the reading voice will ever be heard, that is, out loud.

How we read and how we interpret what we are doing in this act of reading will depend not only on our previous life experiences, but also on how we have been taught to read. A great deal of feminist criticism, both theoretical and practical, is founded on the understanding that "reading as women is not necessarily what occurs when a woman reads: women can read, and have read, as men" (Culler 1982, 49). Implicit in the notion that we read differently according to our gender is the understanding that the experience the reader brings to the text is at least as significant to the interpretation as the reading event itself. Moreover, there are as many experiences as there are readers and no single prerequisite mind-set.

Assumptions about gender provide only one set of criteria for viewing the world, albeit the criteria are significant when we consider how profoundly we are inculcated into our role as male or female. On the other hand, other categories of social organization, such as race and class, are also subject to a dominant reading by a single identifying group. Elizabeth Spelman notes that since "gender is neither experienced nor describable independently of race and class, then race and class become crucial to feminism" (1988, 176). Social and material categories are also crucial to our reading.

The interpretation of any text is never a neutral act in that we can never remove ourselves from our own effective history that predisposes our interpretations. For example, in classes that explicitly teach the interpretation of literature, questions arise about the practice and theory behind the selection of what is going to be interpreted, and who gets to decide. Further, what tradition will be used for the interpretation, and whose purposes are served if things are done in this way? Feminist criticism is one medium for raising questions about the literary and political assumptions on which the reading of texts is based.

What readers of English literature have been trained to value by educational institutions is a male Eurocentric writing aesthetic and the ensuing literary tradition against which all other writing may be judged. Attacks on this literary canon made by the increased visibility of feminist criticism and writing by women and those outside a Western tradition call into question both the aesthetics and the ethics of a literary tradition which cannot verify its claim that its voice is universal.

Reading works by and about women as may be required in doing literary criticism has a parallel in feminist scholarship: both enable women to share common perceptions and "to remove individual women from a sense of isolated personal position" (J. S. Frye 1986, 192). As well, both literary criticism and feminist philosophy engage in questions of women's representation as part of a larger commitment to cultural change. Human experiences take on new meanings as women learn new ways to interpret the lives of other women and of themselves. In a subsequent chapter I will demonstrate how feminist literary criticism acts as both a metaphor for and a real life example of the difficulty of doing a feminist interpretation of texts.

Silencing of women's voices at the university parallels women's historical exclusion from the literary canon (Showalter 1987). The erasure of women's writing from the academy happens as a matter of course when, in spite of the availability of women's literature, it does not make its way into the curriculum. Women's writing has had so little influence on the criteria defining aesthetics and value in a literary work that, in proportion to the number of women writers, the establishment of women's writing in the literary canon has not happened. It is left to each generation of women to discover and reinvent their own tradition, and then watch the influence of women's literature drop like a stone into the sea. Given its availability, the simple discovery of women's writing is clearly not all that is required for it to be accepted into courses of curricular study; women's writing has been rejected on other grounds.

The male domination of interpretive thought found at Canadian universities is indeed pervasive. Such factors as the curriculum, the method of instruction, the sex of the instructor, the organization of the department, and the structure of the university all contribute to the reproduction of the paradigm of Anglo, Western, male, middle-class thought. The issue is not simply one of male-bad/female-good, or to suggest that a feminist interpretation is somehow morally superior. Radical feminism asserts that academia is not only sexist, but also racist, class-biased, and serves an exploitive economic system. In its reproduction of the status quo, academia is incompatible with radical feminism (Gearhart 1983).

Feminist Pedagogy

The interpretation of texts and contexts at the university is nowhere more problematic than in the classroom, where the method of teaching becomes part of the information that is taught. In many ways, the classroom interaction, the structure, and the implicit philosophy is at least as important for the learner as the curriculum. More than an alternative theoretical approach, a feminist pedagogy stands as a critique of the hierarchical structure of academia which reflects on the experience and purposes of one group, thereby giving that group the power to define knowledge. Not only does this hierarchical approach exclude all other definitions, but it limits learning for all people.

A discussion of feminist pedagogy, which will be taken up in more detail in Chapter 4, is not complete without a description of the context in which the teaching will take place. According to Teresa de Lauretis, the problem and struggle of feminist theorizing is "that patriarchy exists concretely, in social relations, and that it works precisely through the very discursive and representational structures that allow us to recognize it" (1984, 165). Locating feminist pedagogy situationally, philosophically, and practically clarifies why it is difficult to carry out and why it meets with such resistance. The onslaught of tradition often defeats revolutionary activity, not necessarily because the ideas themselves do not work, but because the status quo is the main opponent. The new idea, whatever it is, can be labelled as somehow flawed, the proof being its impending demise. In this way, the system justifies and maintains its own ongoing practices. For feminist pedagogy, the issue is not the rightness and truth of a superior method, but the resistance and assumptions that make such a critique necessary and worthwhile.

Overlooking the context in which feminist pedagogy is based leaves these teaching practices open to rejection as just one more fad or well intentioned idea that just did not get off the ground. The problem is not unlike that experienced by any marginalized person whose marginality is socially constructed and yet who is held individually responsible for his or her failure to meet the demands of a repressive system.

It is important to examine ways that pedagogy is carried on at the university because of the profound implications that such an examination reveals about who and what the university serves. Questions about who benefits from the present system may suggest that it is the institution, wider society, business and industry, the discipline itself, or even the students. As with the study of a literary work, the university acts as a text whose message is open to interpretation. I suggest that whatever else it serves now, the teaching in most disciplines at the university rarely serves the students, particularly women students.

Guiding Principles

Two axioms of feminist education are that it is interdisciplinary and that it legitimates life experience as an appropriate subject of analysis or evidence. Both of these principles constitute the matrix of my writing.

The topics I discuss cover a wide range of feminist concerns as they are found in the university context. A partial list of the topics includes research methodologies, women's knowledge, the devaluation of pedagogy, the question of women's authority, methods of literary interpretation, women's representation in texts, the process of pedagogy, specific pedagogical practices, feminist hermeneutics, and feminist poststructuralist analysis. This list illustrates that, like patriarchy, a feminist interpretation of the university is interdisciplinary in nature and is not confined to one method of operation.

You will find that the treatment of the topics listed above is by no means exhaustive, the knowledge as presented here, at best, being partial. These topics do not act as proofs as in a deductive analysis, but as evidence of the reality I am describing. Neither are they linearly connected; instead the topics sometimes overlap and sometimes act as separate themes. The book does not rest on any one of the individual themes, but on their construction of a context for a feminist reading and interpretation.

The second axiom of feminist education—to legitimate life experience as appropriate evidence—is partly accomplished by my inclusion of a personal narrative of my own. I have included journal entries that I recorded in response to a particular series of events that took place during my course of studies. I have placed extracts from the journal at the beginning of each chapter to draw on part of my ongoing engagement with and interpretation of the university experience. As a literary device, the journal acts as a trope in that it stands apart from the body of each chapter and may be compared with and act as an elaboration of the theme. It acts as a frame in which personal experience is an exemplar and a critique. The journal entry, however, also stands on its own, as a narrative and witness of my experience.

The significance of this work lies with its elucidation of feminist pedagogical practices in the context of the masculinist university tradition. The work contributes to feminist theory and practice of education in three ways. First, it performs a feminist interpretation of the university in light of the marginalization of women as women. Second, the work applies a feminist interpretation to an understanding of feminist pedagogy as a hermeneutical process. Third, the work undertakes a reconstructive project by naming some common female experiences in the representation of women at the university. These three activities, repeated throughout the book, are part of both the content and process of the interpretation.

CHAPTER TWO

The University as Text

Journal entry
March 8, 1989

Today I had a terrible experience at the seminar class. It started yesterday and, in a way, it started years ago when I began talking and asking questions. The issue has been with me my whole life as a student and then as a teacher of language—as a person who can't hear words without them appearing before my eyes, sometimes in colour. In some ways I feel like going right to the end and giving the summary, but that isn't being fair to me or to the words and besides, there are too many ends. So I will try to say what happened, happens, is happening.

As a child I wondered about the mysteries of words—meaningless, arbitrary sounds really. But they made sense, not because of themselves alone, but because of what we understood by them. I also knew that words, in fact, pointed to all the things they were not saying, that to say a word was really a joke because behind it stood everything but what was uttered. The only thing words did was represent only those things that were easiest to throw away or could be most easily identified. They came from the excess of what a thing was. It was always understood that they said only those things of least importance—and that the most important parts were yet to come and were always coming. I understood these things as children do and marvelled at the miracle of it—and laughed at my imaginings because no one else was saying it. I laughed because it was either so obvious that no one spoke of it, or else it was so preposterous that no one would listen. But still the words came into my head and told me these things by saying what was not.

In this class on theories of interpretation and the creation of meaning, we have been doing some hard slogging through Heidegger, the Structuralists, Habermas, and now Gadamer. I have had to work hard in this class because my background in analytic philosophy is so very thin. At the same time, I have enjoyed the chance to read about language. Some of the passages in Heidegger are particularly seductive—about how language is a part of us that can't be separated from who we are, about how we call ourselves into being, about how we mediate and are mediated by language. So, as a human being who has thought a lot about this intimate relationship we have with language, I wanted to talk about it in class and have a few things clarified, to trust in the openness of the text that Gadamer elucidates. We were talking about the nature of experience and how we are present in our own effective history. I had many things ready to say.

Yesterday in class I dared to raise the issue of non-rational ways of creating meaning. As usual, I did it right at the end of class, probably so that it wouldn't get much air time, so that I wouldn't have to defend it very long. However, since we were having another class today, the professor said we could bring it up again and encouraged me to do so. He doesn't know that it took every bit of courage to say as much as I did; and that I didn't know if I had any left over for today. But of course I would try.

This morning I got up early to make a few notes. I had done all the readings; I was prepared. But going back was harder because of what I wanted to talk about. I had already said the potentially slanderous words among analytic philosophers: "non-rational" and twice "intuition." Preparing my notes to raise the issue again, I was not unaware of how difficult it would be to discuss these topics adequately among this particular group of men, as difficult as if I had wanted to discuss, for example, a heartfelt belief in UFOs.

I had made copious notes and was very pleased about what I had read. I liked the philosophy that allowed Western tradition to be open to itself—and that science could look at its understanding of how meaning is created—and how there is no way to objectify these sedimented experiences of culture, history, and tradition because they are already part of our present.

Prevailing Norms

The purpose of this chapter is to do a reading of the university text to see what can be learned about some of the very significant activities and ideas promoted there. I suggest that the generation of knowledge through research and scholarship as conducted at the university provides us with a very limited view of what knowledge is and how it is created. Excluded from this narrow view is the work about and by women and other marginalized groups, work that is grounded in both theory and personal experiences. A reading of the university from a feminist point of view results in a critique of the hegemony over meaning which the university upholds.

In reading the university as text, we see that as an educative source of information about personal identity and humanness, the university is a thin read. Instead of learning about critical self-awareness, collaborative and nurturing education, or the social construction of knowledge, we learn the structures of the university to which we must conform in order to be acknowledged as educated persons. The banking concept of education described by Paulo Freire (1974) is well entrenched at universities, in part because of the size of the institutions and the need for efficient production of a learned population. The banking concept, however, suits other agendas at the university as well; it reinforces the existing research paradigm, reproduces the status quo, and supports an accountability modelled after the interests of business and industry.

Notions of student-centred liberatory education espoused by Freire and other critical educators are not generally found at the university, except as topics of a theoretical discussion. Both feminist philosophy and liberatory education begin with learners' points of view and explore how these views evolve in the context of broader social and political relations. In the hierarchical model of the university, this learner-centred characteristic of adult education practice is replaced by a compliance with the structurally imposed requirements faced by both teachers and learners. The capacity of the university to dictate practice and norms is a power which it does not even pretend to share with those involved in the institution. "If institutional education primarily reproduces and nurtures existing power structures, then it cannot possibly be in a position to give power" (Zacharakis-Jutz 1988, 46). University education does not generally promote liberatory or critical notions of power because these are counter to its own elitist structure. The further up the hierarchical ladder of education one moves, the closer one is aligned with the dominant culture. The more rarefied the educational atmosphere, the greater the inertia when it comes to making changes to or criticizing in any way the structure of the institution. The systematizing is so very thorough that years of learned silence cannot be overcome by students who respond to a professor's invitation for dialogue and questions. Rather, systemic distortions require systemic changes.

In the first chapter I discussed the issue of how we read and how our personal experiences influence our interpretation of our reading activity. Our social identification according to race, gender, class, age, sexual orientation, and so forth will be reflected in our reading of the university text. I do not wish to imply, however, that this is a single read, or that all women will have the same perspective simply because we are women. As with other groups, women will hold a myriad of perspectives due to their different histories. In that the experiences of class, race, age, sexual orientation, and other identities are inseparable from the experience of gender relations, I cannot describe a singular women's reading.

Silent Reading

A feminist reading of the male university text speaks of the difference between men and women and of the way women have been fallaciously represented and systemically assimilated into the generic masculine (Schweickart 1986). According to Dorothy Smith (1987a), the key to enlivening the feminist movement is, first, to make central the feminist critique of the dominant ideology at work in our everyday lives; and second, to unveil the ideological nature of values, norms, and beliefs. The values and beliefs of the feminist reading make it inherently critical of the university's support for the status quo, in which being gendered female is a socially created liability rather than an asset (Spelman 1988).

According to Schweickart, the feminist reading of and writing on the university is a site of political struggle. It includes women's claiming of their own experience as a starting point in the project of interpreting the world in order to change it. The reading assumes that the university text is neither cast in stone nor closed to all but the "right" interpretation. Women's articulation of meaning cannot be conflated or reduced to a single voice but can be described, instead, as multivocal. In spite of multivocality, however, the problem remains that women's voices are often not heard at all; women often remain silent, and their questions remain unarticulated. Adrienne Rich describes perfectly the experiences of many women attending university:

> Listen to the voices of the women and the voices of the men; observe the space men allow themselves, physically and verbally, the male assumption that people will listen, even when the majority of the group is female. Look at the faces of the silent, and of those who speak. Listen to a woman groping for language in

> which to express what is on her mind, sensing that the terms of academic discourse are not her language, trying to cut down her thought to the dimensions of a discourse not intended for her. (1979, 243)

If the discourse is not intended for them, why do women attend post secondary institutions? One of the reasons for women's participation is that strategically, attending university is at least as important for women as it is for men. Women have learned that while qualifications alone will not guarantee a career, their chances of employment in anything but a low paying job are slim without a degree. Second, an uncritical look combined with current folklore suggests that at the university, in the pursuit of knowledge and degrees, women will receive fair treatment. Many believe the myth that co-education means equal education (Rich 1977). Gisele Thibault notes the contradiction of women's education. On the one hand, education is a necessary part of the transformation of society; conversely, education systems reinforce the status quo and the structured hierarchy (Thibault 1987). The class structure in society in general is maintained by the educational institution by its inclusion of middle-class women who accept the hierarchical structure of the wider society (Gaskell and McLaren 1987). University historically upholds "the myth that 'education is power' or at least the notion that exposure to knowledge is the panacea of oppression" (Thibault 1987, 179). Further, what the university has not told women is that "the knowledge they have struggled to 'know' is in itself oppressive" (ibid.). Although women are present in numbers, their issues as women are not represented in the text that is the university; they appear only in the margins and footnotes, as part of the research.

The academy's reluctance to include women's knowledge is illustrated by its resistance to the establishment of women's studies classes. These classes threaten the status quo in that women's participation is not limited to the roles of homemaker, care-giver, and educator. Neither are women's efforts confined to a liberal arts education where they are subsumed under the universal rubric "man." Even women's entry into the training colleges dominated by men—where their acceptance is conditional upon their imitation of the male model—is more acceptable and less threatening than women's study of themselves as a sex-class. Even now, the terms "women's studies" and "gender studies" are commonplace, implying a reduction in political potency of the classes that were originally conceived as "feminist studies" (Barry 1991, 83). With a change in name came a change in what were considered acceptable topics for discussion, now reduced in most cases to sexual discrimination and legal inequalities. What became unacceptable were such topics as sexual categories, behaviour, perception, sexual acts, and desire; discussions of sexual politics and power were definitely unacceptable.

Thibault (1987) follows the historic passage of women at the university and divides the barriers to feminist scholarship into three periods. In the first and second periods, feminists were concerned with obtaining equal access, recognition, and pay for women at the university. But as far as hiring practices are concerned, "equal access" has been cloaked in two myths, the first is that colleges and universities are eager to hire and promote women if only qualified women can be found. The second myth, implied by innuendo, is that the women candidates are relatively inferior to males and that the standards will be lowered for a time while women "catch up." That these notions are, in fact, myths (ibid., 60) throws into question the hiring practices that are called objective. In spite of the 1960s and 1970s being a period of great changes in the university, "women . . . gained scarcely 20 percent of the available places during the greatest expansion of higher education in this country" (Hawkins cited in Thibault 1987, 58).

In Thibault's third period, which describes the recent past, feminist dissent goes beyond a concern for parity and asks about the structures and attitudes that make these inequalities so difficult to eliminate. The third stage examines "the ideology which creates and maintains the notion that women are inferior, the institutions which structure male domination and female subordination, and the social sciences which are in many respects, the study of men, by men, for men" (Thibault 1987, 7).

That the university text is not written to include women's experience should surprise no one when we consider how and by whom the academic tradition was established. The preponderance of male faculty and the names on course reading lists and research publications verify that public academic knowledge is created largely by men. Universities simply reflect the traditions, ideas, and thought processes of those who established them, namely, middle- and upper-class men of the white ruling elite. According to Bunch and Pollack, "the higher the step on the administrative ladder, the paler and maler is the atmosphere" (1983, 5).

The silence of women's and minorities' voices in academia is consistent with the university tradition. The practice of the dominant discourse "effected through the humanist tradition has *produced the ideological difference as social inequality*" (Leach and Davies 1990, 325, emphasis in original). In other words, to be different from the tradition is to be unequal to it. Generations of women's enrollment at the university in numbers equal to and greater than men, without an comparable increase in women's influence, attests to the entrenchment of male domination. The only surprising thing is that most of us still accept the assumption that the thought processes of this limited group reflect the thinking of the rest of humanity. The racist, classist, and sexist biases of this assumption are epitomized by the notion that this elitist view has an inherent right ultimately to be the dominant mode of thought.

Creating Norms

Let us look, then, at some of the other underlying ways in which women's needs remain marginalized. This is not automatically an easy thing to do because men and women alike are accustomed to reading the university text from a male point of view. Reading the university text as women brings the readers, first of all, up against the dominant paradigm of research and scholarship at the university. I have chosen to look at research and scholarship because of the central role they play in the definition of the university to the public, to government and business interests, and to the university itself.

Taking a woman's point of view underlines the questions that have for some time been raised about objectivity and value-free research. A feminist critique of science disputes the notion that objectivity is a non-involved stance, claiming instead that, "objectivity is the male epistemological stance, which does not comprehend its own perspectivity" (Thibault 1987, 122). Further claims insist that subjectivity is inherent in all research, regardless of one's epistemological position (Warren 1987; Tomm 1989). The myths of "pure" science and a methodology which is value free are not new topics of discussion, nor are they restricted to women's issues (Kuhn 1970; Freyeraband 1975). The feminist critique notes, however, that the gender bias in research activities largely excludes women's interests, and the knowledge that is produced perpetuates this omission.

Specific examples of sexism and sex blindness in science are identified by Eichler (1988) as follows: overgeneralization in which results of research on men have been generalized for all people (Lawrence Kohlberg's studies (1973) concerned with stages of moral development, in which he used only male subjects, is a case in point); insensitivity whereby women's response in research was not considered to be different from men's; double standards in which identical behaviours of men and women are treated differently by the researcher; giving normative status to social behaviour that has been labelled "proper" according to gender; or treating the sexes as two discrete groups and ignoring their overlap or sameness.

In feminist writing about revisioning the research paradigm, the methodologies proposed are often complex and do not necessarily agree with each other. Research methods that quantify information are not in themselves contrary to women's interests, but an over-reliance on quantitative research methodologies has distorted the general sense of what kind of information is worth collecting. The increasing use of instrumentation to rationalize action, and the strict application of scientific technique locate the research discourse outside of people's everyday experience (Alexander 1991). The problem is that the lives of women have been largely overlooked in the interests of information which is measurable and easy to collect. The ideas of truth and objectivity central to natural science are the embodiment of male norms of objective reasoning, and in this limitation exclude women's experience a priori (Thibault 1987, 120). It is now clear, however, that in order to find out more about women's interpretations, it is necessary to observe their responses and listen to their descriptions, and to have the women themselves ask the research questions. Erroneous assumptions about women have been made because of the lack of attention paid to what women themselves report (Tomm 1989).

By not acknowledging the ways in which one's presuppositions and methods of interacting shape the findings of the research, the researcher is easily lead to false assumptions regarding the subject's reality. In the past, in the search for objectivity, this failure to examine and remove one's influence on the researched subject was simply "bad" science. Now it is recognized that the declaration of one's interests does not remove the interest, and that such presuppositions are not necessarily negative influences if they enable the researcher not only to hear what others say, but also to understand what they mean. This involvement of the researcher with the researched is in keeping with a feminist methodology which rejects the two main assumptions of objective research: that "knowledge of the material world is gained through measurement of natural phenomena," and that the object of study can be isolated from its surroundings (Thibault 1987, 122). On the contrary, one feminist assumption is that a rational explanation includes non-rational factors, and that the notion of an objective measure is largely a reflection of male subjectivity (Tomm 1989).

The reliance on notions of truth and objectivity has placed a rigidity on how we may think about thinking. This rigidity is held in place by science not being self-cleansing or self-regulating and, within its discipline, being cut off from the thinking that would reveal these limitations. Dawn Currie proposes that, to address these limitations, "we treat as problematic the categories of human thought" (1989, 189). Categories of human thought that are particularly problematic include the notion of value-freedom in scientific investigation and the definition of knowledge as either relative or absolute. A radical critique of science, according to Susan Hekman, claims that science is not value-free, but a "socially and politically conditioned activity"; instead of knowledge being defined according to the relative/absolute dichotomy, all knowledge is hermeneutic (1992,135). A feminist critique of the dominant research paradigm emphasizes more than a need to be doing "better" empirical studies, that is, more thorough analysis of women's experience, or the claiming of a standpoint in opposition to all forms of male domination (Harding 1987a). The feminist challenge to science, accompanied by a postmodern critique, is a challenge to the definition of science itself.

A major area of interest in the methodology of feminist research is the inclusion of first-person accounts, especially of women. Men have traditionally been the spokes*men* for human consciousness (McCormack 1983), but feminist approaches are overturning the assumptions about whose knowledge or ways of knowing are acceptable. Perhaps the most important contributions made by the new knowledge about women are the female consciousness that we can now bring to our reading of texts, and the discovery of those texts we did not know existed, including our own.

At the Canadian Women's Studies Association conference in 1993, a woman described her struggle to interpret research interviews she had conducted on a highly introspective topic. She realized she had become "stuck" in her research because she had become involved with and was responding to the data in a way similar to the other interviewees. After much deliberation, she decided to include her own responses and become another research subject, rather than pretend that she had remained unaffected by the research process. The woman's inclusion of her own responses could be interpreted by some as having transgressed the mythical bounds of objectivity; but it is also an example of scrupulous honesty in the process of doing feminist research.

Feminist methodology examines women's lives in a way that makes women the subject of their own experience. Methodology which takes seriously the basic feminist concept that the personal is political cannot permit a separation of the theory about women's lives from the practice of revealing this knowledge. The methodology of consciousness raising is an example of women's collective analysis of their experience and an illustration of one of the ways women come to know more and more about themselves. If we look at consciousness raising as one type of women's research, we can see that this way of creating knowledge, both personal and collective, is an empowering event for women. The discourse and research among women, which is the context of feminist work, is always political and open, never established, finalized, or concluded (Smith 1984, 10). In these collective endeavors, women lay claim to the importance of their partial and particular knowledge.

Tomm (1989) uses an analogy to illustrate loosely the way our knowledge in the past was like the shadows found on the ceiling of Plato's cave (Book VII, *The Republic*). Like the man who escaped to see real objects outside the cave, rather than the reflections on the wall which he thought were real objects, feminists have, in part, escaped the gender-biased groves of academe and have begun to see a new kind of knowledge.

> The problem that contemporary feminists face is similar to that encountered by the man who escaped from the cave. Both have been accused of making claims that are "off the wall." Their new reality is so radically different from that of others that it is difficult to communicate. Their way of knowing has changed to the extent that it is impossible to know as they knew before. (Tomm 1989, 6)

Unfortunately, being labelled "off the wall" works against those who have devised new research directions or theoretical orientations. Under this label, it is difficult to publish unpopular points of view or methodologies in an established field, a difficulty women have noted in their attempts to publish research (CAUT 1988).

Feminist scholarship is inherently critical of the conserving nature of the university and its reproduction of women's oppression in society. The political nature of feminist scholarship differs from most other scholarship in that its politics is overt. The openness of its political intent and the fact that it calls into question the tacit politics of the university system often makes feminist scholarship unwelcome. In any discipline, it can be argued that feminist analysis is the litmus test of academic freedom.

Women's Work

As silent insiders, what can we read from the university text? We see that even though women are visible at the university, they are part of the pyramid of support that places male academic work at the top. Women are associated with the university as sessional lecturers and sometimes as tenured faculty; but more often, women are associated as wives, research assistants, secretaries, teaching assistants, food services personnel, librarians, lower-echelon administrators, or women students. Women's roles at the bottom of the pyramid tend to be defined by their relationship to men in power, instead of to other women up and down the scale (Rich 1979, 137). Rich suggests that "this fragmentation among women is merely a replication of the fragmentation from each other that we undergo in the society outside," and "in its very structure, then, the university encourages women to continue perceiving themselves as means and not as end—as indeed their whole socialization has done" (ibid., 138). This definition of women according to their alignment with men's work and interests pits women against each other and makes it unlikely that they will identify with or respond to their common struggles.

Academic women speak of being hollowed out by their complicity with the patriarchy of the academy. Because they have followed the rules, perhaps critically, but complying nevertheless with at least the official demands of the institutional setting, they are held to account by their sisters who operate outside the walls and reject the elitism perpetuated by the academy. Those outside question academic women's desire and purpose in being there, suggesting that these women have already sold out. Anne Cameron (1989) argues that upper-class academic women should stop presenting papers on and giving interpretations of issues of which they are outside. Their interpretation is no better than a male one, Cameron claims, on topics such as "Welfare Mother Reality" or "Poverty."

At least two points can be raised in a discussion of this issue. One is the uncertainty of whether it is possible for committed feminists to work for change inside an elitist system such as the university. In that system they have likely been irreversibly altered or temporarily deterred from the feminist cause, thus supporting the notion that change of any organization from within is difficult if not unlikely.

Second, women in the academy are cautioned by women outside of it that their efforts to increase the sound of women's voices for gender equity or feminist thought must not be simply an effort to achieve more privilege for women who are already privileged. Feminist discourse is replete with voices that speak with both eloquence and anger about the racism of ignorance and silence among white feminist academics. Whether the university is more sexist than racist is a moot point.

Adrienne Rich (1979) responds to these charges that question the effectiveness of feminist activity in the academy by saying that, among other places, the university is where the students are. Moreover, to begin changes long overdue in academia, women entering the academic professions must bring into the classroom their knowledge of their female experience. Rich cautions against acceptance of academic life at any cost, and urges women to "choose what we will accept and what we will reject of institutions already structured and defined by patriarchal values" (1979, 133).

The cautions against perpetuating the elitism of the academy are important to heed because, among other things, the structural impediments of the academy are designed to pit people against one another. For purposes of hiring and tenure, women are required not only to meet the demands of the system, but also to defend their gender and possibly their race as positive features in the position they hold. Additional structural difficulties confront women academics in their careers. Because their involvement does not always follow the traditional model of their male colleagues, women find their commitment, productivity, and feminist research are evaluated on a different scale (CAUT 1988). Further tensions between the feminist agenda and the academy are created by the paucity of female academics amid a growing interest in feminist scholarship generally, and by women's notable absence from disciplinary content outside of women's studies courses. Although questions often arise about the feminist "bias" of women's studies classes, the absence of any content about women in most other university classes usually goes unmarked as a fair representation of knowledge.

Women's public activities in male dominated fields have long been denigrated. In *A Room of One's Own* Virginia Woolf reports that women's authority in the areas of music and preaching elicited this male response: "it is like a dog's walking on his hind legs. It is not done well, but you are surprised to find it done at all" (1982 [1929], 53). It is quite possible that at the time of Virginia Woolf's writing, in 1928, the same would have been said of women as professors.

The dehumanizing forces of competition are at odds with women's need to support themselves and each other in a system that currently supports elitism and exclusivity. Disciplinary barriers, for example, effectively limit knowledge and isolate women. Within disciplines, knowledge is framed as a product with prescriptive theoretical and methodological means by which reality may be known. The feminist understanding of knowledge—as a social construction—is incompatible with disciplinary approaches which compartmentalize knowledge. Such barriers discourage the reconnection of both knowledge and people, a lack that is particularly hazardous to women as minorities. Isolated by disciplinary barriers and by their low numbers, women students and instructors do not always discover that their problems are not limited to their particular discipline, but are common to women within the institution. Women without a community or support of some kind tend to implode and think their problems are their own fault. Isolated women are being burned out with only the knowledge that they may have made it easier for others. Women need to hear each other, then debate, argue, and affirm what they have in common and recognize where they differ.

Some of the problems that academic women encounter at the university are similar to the ones many women experience in their daily routine: the problems of double duty. As a minority to begin with, women who are professors and who identify themselves as feminist often find their work load especially onerous. Besides a regular teaching assignment, committee work, correspondence, and publishing demands, women are often asked to sit on committees, panels, and boards, to make speeches, and to be visible because they are women; their presence is intended to give the impression of gender equality to publicly organized activities. Especially in fields where women's presence is still an anomaly, women are asked to give *the* female perspective on the particular field, as if women were all the same and their experiences undifferentiated.

If the female academics are feminists, and if they appear at all sympathetic, women students seek them out for personal counselling in areas well beyond academic concerns (Briskin 1990). They hear of women students' experiences of sexual harassment, discriminatory treatment, and rules designed for automatons, but not human beings. Unfortunately, the limited size of the sympathetic audience guarantees that many issues are never raised, and that many women in the face of systemic difficulties remain silent and confused.

Those who are committed to the inclusion of women's experience in their teaching find that, in most disciplines, they could work full time on feminist research alone. Beyond the expectations of traditional research, feminist research requires a rethinking of the role of gender within the discipline, as well as an interrogation of the very structures on which the discipline was erected (Aiken 1988, 108). Feminists find themselves taking on responsibility for their department's feminist research and for meeting the increasingly heavy demands of graduate students for courses on feminist issues. Either implicitly or by fiat, feminists are expected by their departments and their students to solve the problem of gender inequity. The fact that the problem is systemic does not prevent people from looking for and attempting single-handed solutions. If women take on this role of doing the gender housework, their study and critique no longer constitute double duty, but triple. This triple-duty involvement results in a relatively high visibility of women—disproportionate to their numbers and their authority—which serves the university very well. Having the names and faces of women so thoroughly involved in university work helps to spare the university the embarrassment of being publically criticized for hiring so few women. By doing triple duty, the women permit the university community to imagine the presence of women faculty at two, three, and four times their actual numbers.

Feminists in the Classroom

Another problem for female academics centres on the issue of power and authority in the classroom. Here they meet conflicting assumptions based on unexamined traditions and lived reality, both theirs and the students'. In the symbolic order which defines male authority, the denial of women's authority is not changed simply by discursive practices or the recognition that women are also knowledgeable in their fields. If the symbolic order of male domination is not changed, individual and exceptional contributions on the part of women will not change power relations. Even children can see that the one woman who is the exception, "is someone who got her gender relations wrong" (Leach and Davies 1990, 331).

Some of the specific issues concerning women's authority are: first, when expert knowledge is assumed to be inherently male property, how convinced will students be that their equally qualified female instructor is equally expert? Second, should a professor who is committed to interactive education respect the choice of students who wish to remain uninvolved in the learning process and who adopt the role of passive learners? Third, how may professors share their authority with students who do not assume any authority of their own? Fourth, how may a professor share her power with students who are not convinced that, because of her gender, she has any power to share?

Anecdotes persist about what happens to teachers who try to teach from a feminist perspective. Given the general harassment women experience in society in general, it is not surprising that the resistance to overt discussions of feminist issues is swift and sure. Feminists report that they self-censor their lecture material to avoid conflicts with students and other professors (Innis Dagg 1992). One woman reports, "the year after a vitriolic class, I was quite gentle when I taught [that class] the next time. There's only so much blood you can give before you're anemic, and after that it's lights out and you're dead on the floor." Because women often teach in untenured positions, they are particularly vulnerable to negative class evaluations, not to mention the threats, ridicule, and overt hostility frequently expressed by male students (ibid.). The stereotypes of power, intelligence, and authority are so pervasively associated with the masculine that even feminist students report having unequal expectations of male and female teachers (Briskin 1992). Intellectual knowledge alone does not easily overcome socialization that permits males to exact high standards and discipline and alternately pressures women teachers to provide nurturance and unconditional approval (ibid.).

Briskin (1990) reports on the difficult balance facing feminist professors who attempt to equalize the power relationship in their classes by giving up their institutionalized authority. In her studies this movement towards a more democratic classroom, which is rarely an easy transition for anyone, is perceived quite differently depending on the professor's gender. Students perceive that more democratically constructed classrooms taught by female professors indicate that the women are unsure of themselves and lack credibility; conversely, male feminists suffer from an embarrassment of riches. Students adopt overtly subordinate roles and constantly look to the male professors for verification and approval of what they have learned (ibid.).

Because of their gender, female academics often emphasize grounds for credibility which may not be a concern for men. When I spoke separately with three feminists about their classroom practices, I noticed some differences that were at first puzzling to me. One professor was concerned about the high academic standards she set. She required that students cover as much as possible on a particular feminist topic and emphasized that students needed a firm grasp of the material in order to participate meaningfully in the discussions. A second woman believed dialogue was very important in feminist classes and spent a lot of energy engaging students in this activity. The third feminist, a man, did not articulate theories of teaching; he merely told me what he did. His feminist approach was intuitive, practical, and concerned simply with how best to help the students learn.

I mention these conversations because I was surprised by the calm with which the man described his teaching. He surely covered less material and frequently worked through problems with students who were in open disagreement with him. But, by sharing his power with students, they all became co-learners. I believe that such a relaxed approach has at least as much to do with his individual personality as it does with being male, and that his power to divest and bestow authority is a luxury that women academics can not so easily afford.

How is the feminist pedagogue to position herself in the classroom? My struggle with how to answer this question with respect to racism made me realize that, as a white woman in a classroom of white students, the feminist position is truly a fragmented one. A comment from a white, male colleague that, in this regard, I should simply be myself was both unhelpful and ironic. As a white feminist, my racial identity locates me with the dominant group. That is to say, in the institution where I teach the colour of my skin goes unnoticed; as the unmarked norm. The same, however, is not true of my gender. As part of my identity, my positions of gender and race are in constant negotiation with the ideological constraints and interactions of my social context. Susan Heald (1991) sheds light on this situation when she discusses her situatedness and how it is her gender that marks her as other in the classroom. I, like her, have various constructed identities; the effect being that I cannot assume a singular subject position or know for certain which self to be. Nor am I free to determine which constructed identity will matter in a particular instance. Even though I enter the discourse of teaching as a white female of working-class background who is heterosexual and able-bodied, my class background and race are not made an issue in the mostly white, middle-class institution where I teach. The context and discourse of the university have already outlined the identity of the person who will pass through the classroom door. That outline takes the shape of a white male or anyone else who can or is willing to conform to the norms set by this dominating figure.

Devaluation of Pedagogy

Feminist concerns about education and their insistence on congruence between theory and practice challenge traditional operating methods at the university. Feminist perspectives call for a change in the framework of scholarship generally, not merely for the addition of women or a body of research about women (Dubois, Kelly, Kennedy, Korsmeyer, and Robinson 1985), because the "add women and stir" approach (Bunch and Pollack 1983) implies that the existing information is unproblematic. An important feminist challenge to academic research is over the importance attached to "having knowledge" as opposed to "ways of knowing," the latter being characteristic of many feminist approaches. Furthermore, I believe that the importance placed on research results in it overshadowing equally important endeavors carried out at the university, particularly teaching.

When advancement depends on one's publications and the ability to secure grants, teaching is relegated to an occasional or incidental activity (Wilshire 1990). Professors are rarely relieved of their research load so they can devote their time to teaching, but the reverse is not unusual: for a full professor, the lighter the teaching load, the greater the prestige (ibid., 78). In the hierarchy of the university, those who perform teaching duties only, are hired to marginalized positions as sessional lecturers. Not surprisingly, the number of women faculty generally increases as status of the position decreases.

The professionalization of education proceeds from elementary to secondary schools and reaches its epitome at university levels. In this movement from elementary to graduate level teaching, two corresponding shifts occur. First, the number of women teachers decreases, and second, an emphasis on the process of knowledge gives way to an emphasis on the possession of knowledge. Disregard for education as a process is clearly shown when the most highly professionalized teachers may achieve those ranks by the knowledge they possess rather than their ability to teach. So undervalued is the ability and knowledge of how to teach that the ranks of the professoriat may be achieved without any pedagogical instruction whatsoever. This is not to set up a false dichotomy between professional education training and one's intuitive sense of what is the right thing to do in the classroom. The notion that these are opposites devalues both the skill and art of teaching possessed by both women and men. However, with the possibility that the best teaching is being done in elementary schools, one cannot help but notice that, as far as institutional qualifications are concerned, the highest degrees of professionalization are inversely related to the value placed on quality teaching.

Professionalization of education, in which knowledge is truly a bankable commodity, is at odds with what Noddings calls a feminine view. "It is feminine in the deep classical sense—rooted in receptivity, relatedness, and responsiveness" (1984, 2). That is not to say that logic is to be discarded or that this feminine view is an essential quality of women and one that is alien to men, although it is an approach that one is taught to expect among women rather than among men. Johnson also notes that in the discussion of feminist issues, there is a move "to reverse the impersonalization ... and to reintroduce the personal, or at least the positional, as a way of disseminating authority and decomposing the false universality of patriarchally institutionalized meanings" (1987, 44).

The notion of receptivity and the ethic of caring are rooted in the particular in a concept of justice which sees the person for whom the principles of justice were formed, and not just the principle itself (Gilligan 1982). In contrast to rule-based, generalizable justice, the feminine notions of justice are person-centred and particular (Friedman 1987). The latter approach singles out justice as more than an abstract virtue rationalized to mean equal treatment for all people. Insofar as people are not equally interchangeable, the concept of equal justice depends on the individual and the particular. Feminism is committed to a social view of justice that pays attention to the specific and the personal. It is in caring for the other that feminism stands against injustice.

The feminist commitment to the notion that the personal is political does not accept the mind/body split inherent in traditional pedagogy. For feminists, curriculum and teaching strategies are both politically significant for deconstructing the hierarchical structures of academe. A person-centred education, and especially the articulation of women's experience as a source of knowledge, are not what we now see when we read the university. Historical and present day resistance encountered by women and other marginalized groups to an expanded view of experiential knowledge and practice cannot be explained simply by the inertia of an unwieldy system. Resistance avoids the risk that "objectivity will be revealed as itself value-laden, serving the interests of male (and class) superiority; as do the concepts of rationality, justice, equality, freedom, knowledge, [and] progress" (Miles and Finn 1989, 226).

In a setting in which only objective, public knowledge is permitted, the good scholar has been encompassed by the definition of a good scientist (Raymond 1985, 58). The feminist interpretation of knowledge confirms the worth of each person's experience, and thereby reflects the pluralistic, historical, and contextual nature of human society. Knowledge cannot be defined by a single group, but must be interpreted and created by multiple groups for there to be an understanding and representation of their lives (Maher 1985, 35).

In this chapter, I have discussed the representation of women in the context of the university, a place which, on the one hand, espouses values such as academic freedom, collegiality, democratic decision making, meritocracy, and the notion of education as a leveller. On the other hand, we see that these values are defined in terms of a class system designed for and by patriarchy. The system is not different from the one which operates to support the status quo and its economic values in wider society. It is a formulaic process that is number driven—its qualitative benefits determined by quantitative assessment. This class system is hierarchical and assumes that the initial distribution of authority is just. Rather than supporting analysis or criticism of existing practices, people in positions of power perceive the structures and forces which bring them privilege as part of the natural order of things.

The effect of this discrepancy between espoused values and their practice is not simply marked by loss of human potential and utility, but by the lack of justice in a leading, public institution. Although a putative leader of society, the university has become a reluctant follower in the move to dismantle the systemic barriers that limit access to full expression of human rights and dignity.

CHAPTER THREE

Feminist Pedagogy and English Literature

JOURNAL ENTRY

Finally this morning's session took place. In my notes I starred the things that seemed important. There were lots of stars. The discussion went the same way as always: I was mute. I have tried to discover why I was silent and have concluded a few things. First, I wanted to say things that weren't very popular, like "non-rational" and "intuition" (at least UFOs are not a gender-biased topic). Second, I wanted to talk about my own experiences because that is how I understood the text. Third, I wanted others to do a synthesis rather than abstract analysis. Fourth, the others were all men who had extensive backgrounds in philosophical arguments—statement of proposition followed by counter proposition or an analysis backed by statements of authority.

I didn't want to ask or suggest that there was another way (or several) for the class to happen, partly because the topic was too important for me to expose my feelings about it, and partly because I didn't want them to "go along" with my suggestion for a while and then go back to abstractions because "that is how you really talk about it." The other reason I didn't ask was because I didn't think I could say the words with my heart in my mouth.

I left at the break and said I had to go to work. I know it isn't entirely my problem that I didn't say anything, but still I operate from the premise that I have to adjust my thinking about the topic to suit the dominant discourse, and that it can't be the other way around because after all they're not running a therapy session.

> *And it's my problem if I'm so emotional that I can't say anything. The real issue is made clearer, however, by the fact that the rest of the class (the men), are all fairly nice people who wouldn't have interrupted me and may even have welcomed what I wanted to say. It was not just a matter of courtesy and although the men may not be personally to blame, they are part of the problem. The discourse of the university favours them by reflecting their understanding and knowledge in a way that corroborates their right to be there. I know that is how the tradition is supposed to operate, but I wanted somehow to find a way to learn things that are more authentically who I am. Instead, I was silenced about a topic which is of great importance to me. Ironically, this is International Women's Day.*
>
> *What was most distressing was that in the text itself there was a discussion about this very point: that consciousness of standing in our traditions is what makes it possible to know and talk about those traditions. In the face of this invitation, the seminar examined neither the traditions of the university, nor the nature of discourse, nor the hegemony of Western thought, but used its privilege to talk, theoretically, about something completely different.*

Introduction

In this chapter I look at the interpretation of texts as a form of power that reveals a culture's ideology and aesthetics. Decisions about who writes and who gets to interpret the text tell less about the texts than they do about whom and what the dominant ideology supports. This chapter continues the discussion of the university context as a site for the placement of feminist theorists and their positioning as interpreters, speakers, and writers.

One of the main points of contention, as discussed in Chapter 2, has been the extent to which scientism and the notion of objectivity dominate the research paradigm and, by extension, the criteria of what counts as knowledge. In a similar way, a decontextualized, objectified method of interpretation in English literary criticism, like an objectification of the natural world, also distorts the literary landscape. Unfortunately, in the case of New Criticism, a force which continues to influence undergraduate literary pedagogy (Lentricchia 1990), the interpretation is achieved by excluding values, history, social conditions, and personal motivations of writers. Generations of readers have learned to subordinate their active participation with the text and to humble themselves "before the 'creative' authority of a superior primary writing" (ibid., 324). By examining how a literary discourse is structured, we can see what values are supported and what effect each discourse produces; furthermore, what difference does the bias of each discourse make? The purpose of this third chapter is to locate more specifically the difficulty that this hegemonic notion of value-free interpretation creates for feminist literary criticism and the production of women's writing.

I discuss in more specific ways the difficulties feminist pedagogy and modes of thought face when situated in a particular academic discipline. As before, I am not discussing the specifics of how this pedagogy is to be carried out, but rather, I illustrate that like the university structure, the activity of specific disciplines is similarly gendered. Rather than studying one of many disciplines which would quickly illustrate the difficulty of introducing feminist thinking, I have chosen the one that I think is among those most receptive, that is, English literature. The question in any discipline, however, is whether women can claim to have their own voices without succumbing to the pitfalls of essentialism, whether biologically, socially, or metaphysically determined.

I also discuss ways in which English literature as a discipline at the university is a prime example of scholarship dominated by analytical thought and reasoning to the distrust and exclusion of human experience and response. This section parallels the discussion in the previous chapter in which a feminist critique of science questions that discipline's claim to locate truth through objectivity. Similarly, various influential schools of literary criticism declare meaning in literature and in society by standing behind unassailable terms of self-reference. In this chapter, I first discuss how often-used types of literary criticism typically exclude thinking that departs from the declared meaning of the English literary paradigm in ways that limit what we may describe as knowledge. I also describe how it is difficult for women to establish a place to begin speaking as writers, given their relegation to a position of "other" in literature. What is women's place in writing in the gap between the clichés about women and their self-representation? With some understanding of the need for a description of the poststructural, nonessential subject, this chapter concludes with a discussion of women's aesthetic and women's voice.

I chose English literary criticism to "read" as opposed to some other discipline for three reasons. First, as an art form, English literature is experience-based and, supposedly, more in touch with the subjective, non-rational, creative world than, say, history or geology. Literature offers a range of understandings of human development and thinking in ways not readily accessible through sciences that rely on sense perceptions. A literary artist who begins from personal experience and makes that experience public, portrays "themes of human experiences in ways that allow us to understand and to see our own lives with greater clarity and order" (Merriam 1983, 6). One quality of a literary work is that, in narrating something of what it is to be human, it reveals the experience for a particular culture according to that culture's codes of behaviour, representation, and interpretation. Feminist pedagogy also recognizes the importance of personal experience for understanding and creating theory; like English literature, it is grounded in a fragmented set of practices and possibilities which we first experience and then describe.

My second reason for looking at the discipline of English literature is the large number of women who choose to study English compared to, for example, engineering or mathematics. My focus is not whether as a university subject, English literature has been affected by the large numbers of female students, although my study suggests that high numbers of women, alone, do not outweigh the preponderance of traditional thought in the disciplines. Rather, using the discipline of English literary studies as my specific field of research, I demonstrate how pervasive and inappropriately located is the tendency to treat knowledge as something to be schematized and structured. Even in a discipline that uses as its subject matter accounts of the human condition, objectivity and abstract thought replace that which is personal and specifically located. We must look elsewhere for why it is that women make up a large portion of students and a small portion of faculty, or why women form the majority of readers and men the majority of writers.

The third and perhaps most important reason for choosing to study English literature, particularly literary criticism, is its hermeneutical function. Hermeneutics is central to the humanities' task of interpreting the experiences and works of humanity. In the Western philosophical tradition, primacy of meaning resides in interpretations of the word and in the construction of reality from discourse. The interpretation of texts and contexts is at the centre of the most powerful cultural influences in the Western world: religion, law, and academic learning. The church, the judicial system, and the university, through their studies of the word, claim and are awarded the authority and power to define interpretation and meaning in the context of their area of concern and in society. Typically, English literature represents the study of theories of interpretation which inform and are informed by the philosophies from which this discipline is constructed. In choosing English literature and its task of textual interpretation, I do not undertake an analysis of its domination as an interpreter, but rather of the capacities of various interpretations to represent women's experiences. I have chosen feminist constructivism as a basis for the interpretation of texts and for discussing women's position in the construction of meanings in literature.

The Wish to Ape Science

It comes as no surprise that English literature, as a university discipline, is interpreted on the basis of a male-dominated construct. Being an art form, English literature experiences an even greater need to assert its masculinist qualities in order to claim its place as a discipline alongside the sciences and the professional training programs of the university. The late, pre-eminent Canadian literary scholar, Northrop Frye, remarks that compared to the physical sciences which are so symbolically male and out in the world doing things, literature is "narcissistic, intuitive, fanciful, staying at home and making the home more beautiful, but not doing anything serious and therefore symbolically female" (1975, 201). To shore up literature against such dubious associations, his *Anatomy of Criticism* (1957) attempts to make the study of literature more serious and manly by structuring its principles scientifically like the laws of physics, biology, or mathematics (Showalter 1987).

The exclusion of women's influence from the interpretation of English literature is somewhat surprising given that literature is an art form reflecting the human condition. The effect of women's exclusion can easily lead us to believe that the human condition by default, is male. Clearly, the conflation of masculinity with authority as a characteristic of our society is seen as a culturally acceptable condition (J.S. Frye 1986; Dubois et al. 1985).

Alarm bells and exhortations caution English literary studies to return to the literary works themselves as the focus of investigation, as opposed to the preponderance of studies about the works. Literary criticism and analysis are comparable to the pure research counterpart of the natural sciences. Those who have shaped the discipline of literature to what it is today have worked hard to protect its status against its early associations with subjects suitable for study by young women entering institutions of higher learning (Pope 1989). Now, the investigation of theories, assumptions, and hypotheses, and the accompanying publication of the findings, is not unlike the production of explanations and theories in many other disciplines, including the sciences.

Benstock (1987) says that objective aesthetic distance is not only undesirable, it is also impossible. The dissection of literature as if it were an aesthetic machine denies the social, political, and historical culture of which it is a part. She continues on to say that

> literature must not be seen in the dichotomous view of the male scientist as an "it" opposed to the "I" of the analyst. Nor must literature be seen as a transcendent string of disembodied masterpieces that are disconnected from their specific historical socio-

> cultural locale. Literature, communities, critics, and authors must be seen as bound up in a relational network. Just as modern physics recognizes that reality is contingent upon the positional relativity of the observer, so must modern criticism reject the Newtonian notion of critical objectivity. A women's epistemology, as identified by modern theorists, is appropriately contextual and relational. (ibid., 106-7)

Literary scholarship has a way of escaping the experience of the literary work when, instead of suggesting that we read the work, it asks how we will deal with it (Barzun 1984). To the extent that literature becomes the property of professionals and their scholarship, knowing what one thinks about the subject becomes infinitely more important than direct experience with it. My uncomfortable experience in the philosophy class I mentioned in the journal entry that begins this chapter resulted from the same confusion. I was inexperienced with the correct method for discussing the particular text. I had not, however, failed to understand the work itself or to form conclusions about it. Ironically, the text under discussion was on the nature of how one experiences art. The discussion was completely in the abstract, as if the class wanted to avoid admitting that they had ever experienced art.

The most prestigious academic labour remains rooted in the abstract and the theoretical, which rarely gives even a passing reference to one's experience with the text, even in the reading of it. When the unquestioned aim becomes analysis of the work, the discussion of method flowers as the focus of debate. Richard Palmer says that in the common-sense objectivity of literary criticism, which has become increasingly technological, the act of analysis is seen as synonymous with interpretation. He insists that neither a scientific way of knowing nor a disinterested objectivity is appropriate for literary interpretation. "Dialogue, not dissection, opens up the world of a literary work" (1969, 7).

Perhaps some of the most extreme examples of English literature under analysis are found in the work of Northrop Frye, who believes that the interpreting of literature is untouched by the history of human experience. He suggests that "literary criticism is a pseudo-scientific approach that operates *beyond* taste, value judgements, and the uniqueness of an artist and his work" (Powe 1985, 37). Frye's greatest contribution to literary theory is his belief in a closed universe of structure, myths, and character types (Lentricchia 1990, 325) in which literature is maintained as an "imaginary alternative to modern society" (Eagleton 1983, 93). Free of the sordidness of the material world, literature is left to generate literature. By setting up his self-sustaining organizational framework for literature, Frye is able to ignore the historical forces that privilege certain canons of writing.

The wish to ape science and to rely on its tools of analysis, proof, and method has created a literary criticism in which responses must be measured by and limited to the use of these tools (Grant 1969). My point, however, is not to question the efficacy of research itself, but to problematize the closedness of many types of research, the question of whom or what is served by the investigation, the assumptions made about knowledge, and the domination of research over the real life event. Feminists such as Nina Baym (1987) are also critical of feminist literary theory because it is grounded in theories such as deconstruction or Marxism that are indifferent to women's writing and are "irretrievably misogynist." She charges that theory becomes just another way to divide women and serves only as a means of legitimation for women in the audience of prestigious male academics.

On the other hand, there is an important place for feminist literary theories which critique patriarchal structures and speculate from a women's point of view how, why, and under what assumptions women have come to occupy the role of the oppressed. Women need to develop theory to reflect and describe women's writing and pedagogical practices. Like women's presence at the university in general, women's work in literature studies is attributable to the pleasure some take in studying, teaching, or writing; pleasure which may be either a natural response to curiosity or a learned response which has become intrinsically satisfying. This is not a gendered kind of pleasure, but one that is open to women as it is to men. While feminists at the academy are aware of the gender bias of the curriculum and of the ideological positioning of the institution, they are also aware that their presence is a statement of their right to claim their own pleasure.

Paraphrasing Virginia Woolf in *Three Guineas*, Rich says that the more crucial task for women at the university is the process of deciding on what terms we will participate in "the procession of the sons of educated men" (1979, 132). I first discuss the tradition which a feminist literary analysis enters when it starts the process of participation in the historically and culturally significant area of the interpretation of texts.

The Arbitrary Nature of Objectivity

I have already tried to show how claims of objectivity in the process of interpretation are impossible to support. First, every theory supports some political agenda and simply declaring it to be neutral and universal does not make it so. Second, the value of objectivity is itself questionable, as it is in science, as what cannot be explained is simply excluded. The claim of objectivity and the "myth of disinterest" serves only to provide an argument for the exclusion of theories, such as feminist literary criticism, which acknowledge that they are historically situated, and part of a continually shifting and changing social and cultural context (Pope 1989).

Feminist literary criticism as a theory of interpretation is located within the discipline of English literature among other theories of interpretation such as formalist, New Criticism, phenomenology, reception theory, structuralism, poststructuralism, psychoanalysis, and political theory, to name only a few. These are relatively recent theoretical constructions compared to the traditional beginnings of hermeneutical interpretation which scholars originally applied only to religious texts. The interpretation of religious texts has its own history in which one "comprehensive" theory replaces another over the years.

Terry Eagleton (1983) shows that the basis of an interpretation theory is determined by a wider arena than literature alone, that theories are informed and sustained by certain readings of social reality. In this interpretation process, the study of literature essentially involves describing a large, amorphous body through focusing on the part that seems most salient because of the particular interpretation being applied. Each methodology subsumes what it thinks is important for the interpretation of literature, and whatever gets left out is, by definition, unimportant.

From a feminist perspective, a discussion of the merits of various literary theories must make problematic what is to be considered as literature. On what terms will writing about and by women be included? In particular, what roles will women play as writers beyond the marginalized positions now offered, and how may the characters be interpreted; what will reading be like when it is acknowledged to be a gendered activity? Eagleton states that new definitions of literature do not simply provide ever differing accounts of, for example, the plays of Samuel Beckett. He suggests that a redefinition or "breaking with the literary institution . . . means breaking with the very ways literature, literary criticism and its supporting social values are defined" (ibid., 90). Below, I provide a brief discussion of the codes and structures by which some literary theories operate.

According to formalist criticism, literature is a special kind of language and a function of the differential relations between one sort of discourse and another (ibid., 4). What is named as literature is identified by its special use of language as, to give a clear example, in the case of poetry. In formalist criticism, features of the work are examined and described in isolation from biographical, historical, psychological, or intertextual considerations. This exclusive focus on language as the defining characteristic of what is called literature means that only by inclusion in a literary genre can language be judged as literary (ibid.). The problem with this, of course, is that expressions used in a novel and defined as literary may be indistinguishable as literature when the same words are used in ordinary conversation.

Two other theories which illustrate the specialized nature of literary criticism have opposing principles—New Historicism and the doctrine of death of the author. New Historicism requires that readers are aware of the historical conditions under which a work was first produced, published, and read in order for them to have a full appreciation of the significance of the work. On the other hand, Roland Barthes (1972) argues that the meaning of a work is dependent on the structure of the language and is completely independent of the author's intentions and meaning. In death of the author, the task of the criticism is to unlock the multitude of possible "meanings" that the text alone can generate—the self-referential language of literary criticism is found to be sufficient for this type of analysis.

Reader-response is one theory that self-consciously permits the entry of personal values into its analysis. In this process the reader acknowledges and emphasizes his or her participation in both the reading of the work and in the analysis of the literary process. In refusing to function only on the level of theory, reader-response admits other facets of human reality such as science, history, politics, a variety of psychologies, the facts of literary creation, the sociology and economics of the professor, and so forth. But even though the reader-response theory offers a way to return both literature and life to literary studies, it offers students no leverage from which to critique their own assumptions about literature. As Eagleton says of reader-response, "what you get out of the work will depend in large measure on what you put into it in the first place, and there is little room here for any deep-seated 'challenge' to the reader" (1983, 80). Similarly, "the closedness of the circuit between reader and work reflects the closedness of the academic institution of Literature, to which only certain kinds of texts and readers need apply" (ibid.).

A question that reader-response is unable to ask is what difference it would make to the experience and meaning of literature if the reader were a person of colour, poor, and/or female. In its inability to critique, reader-response can only assume an objective text and gender-neutral criticism. Coming from a liberal-humanist tradition, this theory intends to be neutral, but results in supporting the status quo.

The point, however, is not simply to dismiss certain literary theories by countering them with other, presumably better, ones. It is important to see that literary theories are social constructions that come from certain social ideologies that are also expressed in philosophy, linguistics, psychology, and other studies (Eagleton 1983). The concern is over what is to be considered as literature, and that what is considered great depends on who is in a position to authoritatively declare "greatness" (Pope 1989). To qualify as a topic of literary discourse and criticism, a work must first be judged as literary; however, entrance into this ring is determined by the literary institutions (Eagleton 1983, 89).

The problem that this closed-circuitry presents for women's writing, feminist literary criticism, and feminist pedagogy is that the norms and definitions of what is aesthetic have already been decided, with a most noticeable lack of input by women. In literary history, popularity and greatness have been separated, and the latter has been shaped by "the attitudes, conscious or unconscious of white men towards nonwhites and nonmales" (Bernikow cited in Pope 1989, 31). The concern is that women's voices in English literature are acceptable only if they meet these culturally assigned aesthetic values. The centrality of this privileging is one of the reasons the feminist project makes problematic the areas of reading and writing, as these are crucial components for "interpreting the world in order to change it" (Schweickart 1986, 39). Pope continues,

> feminist criticism is inevitably connected to the most fundamental considerations of culture and cultural institutions, and brings a new scrutiny and skepticism to bear on such professionally powerful concepts as tradition, the canon, and standards of excellence, and shows how under the rhetoric of *universal*, these concepts have meant *nonfemale*. (1989, 27)

Pope (1989) says that the gendered nature of literary criticism is also visible in the distinction between popular readers and those who are trained; between material that is accessible and that which is privileged and in need of instruction; and between an emotive stance and an intellectual one. Of course, the popularity of a work is its death-knell—a popular work is more likely to be labelled "common" than literary.

Feminists have pointed out that the prevailing canon and literary theories exclude, marginalize, and stereotype women's participation as characters, readers, writers, and interpreters. In the literary tradition, women's values, experiences, and aesthetics, as reported by women, are all but silenced. The plethora of diverse feminist literary criticisms all find problematic the assumptions about both literature and women that have resulted in the distorted and silent representation of women in the canon. Without this challenge to cultural norms, modern critical theories, including post-structuralism, are inadequately equipped to discuss issues concerned with literary value and evaluation (Showalter 1987).

Modern literary and critical theories are far from being value free or neutral. On the contrary, their silence on the question of women's issues already demonstrates the value that to be human is to be male. In their treatment of value judgements as non-issues, they remain as self-referential as any positivistic science. The objectivist suppression of non-rational qualities such as value, sentiment, empathy, and emotion, and elevation of the rational, assumes that words alone can be used to construct a reality, "fashioned by particular people for particular reasons at a certain time" (Eagleton 1983, 11). The theories are historically variable and have a close relation to social ideologies of the particular time.

The assumption of critical objectivity is not simply a matter of how texts are defined; it is "the assumption by which certain groups exercise and maintain power over others" (ibid., 16). "Literary interpretation is a political act and like the politics of anything else, the main issue is power" (Fetterley 1978, 4).

The extent to which masculinity and authorship merge in a culturally acceptable authority has been at the expense of a female definition of authorship in anything other than masculine terms (J.S. Frye 1986; Fetterley 1978). The peculiar form of powerlessness is not simply due to the erasure of efforts or the silencing of voice, nor is it the lack of recognition or legitimation of one's art. The powerlessness comes more significantly from the endless division of "self against self, the consequence of the invocation to identify as male while being reminded that to be male—to be universal . . . is to be *not female*" (Fetterley 1978, xiii). "Forced in every way to identify with men, yet incessantly reminded of being woman, she undergoes a transformation into an 'it,' the dominion of personhood lost indeed" (ibid., ix).

Because success and authority are defined in male terms, women readers, teachers, and scholars do not necessarily find it easy to read outside of the encoded interpretation strategies. By accepting as normal and legitimate a male system of values, the *immasculation* of academic women is accomplished (Fetterley 1978). Their bifurcated response and self-surveillance follows directly from the fact that the reality of patriarchy is constructed both inside and outside the reader. The representation of women in literature is not different from what happens in other art forms, such as in visual representations, when it is the male viewer's gaze that defines women. Again women are split in the way they simultaneously watch themselves and watch men watching them as objects. As John Berger says of visual representation, "men act and women appear" (1972, 47). Male control of textuality, even when women write, means that men never have to endure the gaze as "other." By firmly controlling self-enhancing readings, men can avoid the alienating readings they have allotted to women (Fetterley 1978). "The female body is neither neutral or natural; it is clearly inscribed in a system of differences in which the male and his gaze hold power" (Hutcheon 1989, 155).

A feminist literary theory has, as one part, a critique of theories that continue such exclusionary practices as determining in advance what will be included. Feminist literary criticism makes problematic the way interpretation theories have underestimated, derided, or ignored women's point of view in literature. The critique also extends to methodology that does not acknowledge the political nature of its organizing practices.

Feminist literary criticism, however, is more than a critique of men's studies. It begins with experiences of reading a text from a women's point of view. The point of view locates experiences in social constructs which are also part of the reading. The readings make the experiences problematic by revealing how they relate to material social practices in women's lives and to the power relations which structure the experiences both inside and outside the text.

In representations of their experiences, male and female experiences of reality are valued differently. In using the written word, it is the medium of fiction that remains available to women, and women's reality is mainly revealed not only *in* but also *as* fiction. Other genres that women often use, such as journals, diaries, and letters, are often discounted as literature because they cannot be written off as fiction. Men's fiction, however, can be read in the law, the universities, the churches, and the civil and moral codes by which our society is ordered. Male subjectivity and men's stories of their own world and the world of others has created this version of reality. In contrast, because they are recorded as fiction, women's accounts of their own reality need not be believed (Brossard interviewed in Daurio 1991, 20). The accounts of women remain available for those who know how to read them.

An example of women's reading of each other's lives is found in the short story, "A Jury of her Peers," by Susan Glaspell (1916). In this story, some women accompany their husbands who have come to investigate the motive for the murder of a local farmer at the hand of his wife. The woman's guilt is established, but the motive remains unclear; without a motive, there can be no conviction. While the men on their official business search elsewhere, the visiting women occupy themselves with the guilty woman's world of the kitchen. There the women read telltale signs of an unhappy life revealed in the apparently meaningless disorder of the woman's kitchen. The subtle disarray has meaning which speaks to those who know how to read. The men return from their unfruitful search for a motive and chide their wives for their womanly preoccupations of quilting and housekeeping. The story, when told in its completeness, exemplifies women's exclusion from the search for truth and reveals how women's culture is "invisible, silenced, trivialized, and wholly ignored in men's construction of reality" (Andersen 1988, 37). The story also exemplifies how women can read the effects of their experiences in the representation of other women's lives.

A woman's writing that most recently reflected my life is that of Anne-Louise Brookes (1992). She is an academic who found it increasingly difficult to write until she was able to acknowledge that she had been a victim of abuse. She talks about "absenting" herself from discourse or withdrawing psychologically to a private place where she could not be hurt. In withdrawing, she also lost her public voice and when she wrote at all, her personal voice remained completely absent. A person who has been degraded by someone in authority loses the sense of self that she could otherwise use to defend her against authority figures. Similarly, I absented myself from the seminar class I write about in my journal, and physically withdrew when I realized that my language was not satisfactory for discussing something I was very enthusiastic about. I did not realize all of this at the time, but later put together the pattern of silent attention I had paid in classes, lectures, and before male authority figures who dominated discussions as if they were endlessly interesting. By comparing it to my own, I do not wish to trivialize Brookes' experience which she kept painfully secret for so many years. My experience of powerlessness before male authority, however, also took place over many years, and it was so normal it could even occur in public. The seminar class was significant, but it is only one example of how the reasonableness of authority and the orthodoxy of institutions have worked to silence me. When I took a step back from the seminar class, I saw that the basis for excluding the majority of people who were not represented had nothing to do with intelligence. The non-male and non-white majority would, quite correctly, not have recognized the discourse as their own, and would have found its criteria of exclusion arbitrary at best. In Brookes' autobiographical writing, my own process became clearer to me.

In the experiences of others expressed in literature, women can read their own lives. Indeed, the reason why some women become feminists is not because they have necessarily read something new or learned new facts, "but they have come to view those facts from a different position, from their own position as subject" (Alcoff 1988, 286). Reading the text as a woman is a profoundly important step toward a feminist interpretation of texts.

Feminist scholarship has added to notions of what is literary by considering the wide range of genres in which women write. Robinson suggests that "women's letters, diaries, journals, autobiographies, oral histories, and private poetry have come under critical scrutiny as evidence of women's consciousness *and expression*" (Robinson cited in Showalter 1985, 117). Women's writing challenges the canonical definitions of the literary aesthetic and the limitation of forms in which literature may be found by "measuring literature against an understanding of authentic female life" (Donovan 1989, 46). The development of a feminist poetics emerges not simply as a definition of women's experience in literature, but as a "shared inquiry into the understanding of female experience and its relationship to literature" (ibid., 17).

Women's Knowledge: Apart or A Part

The discussion which follows is more than a philosophical argument about speaking and writing; it highlights practical concerns about whether women can participate in such events as writing novels, writing literary criticism, teaching at a university, or being a student without being absorbed into the sameness of masculinist constructions. The argument known as the sameness/difference debate in feminist philosophy has long been described as dated, boring, and a concept women struggled with before they discovered poststructuralism. While the debate may be all of these things in a philosophical sense, it continues to have practical relevance for predicting some of the pitfalls and institutional traps facing feminist literary criticism. Conceptualized more broadly, on the sameness side of the debate, are women's issues and feminist philosophy to be seen merely as yet another good idea; the alternate question being whether women are to claim status only in their difference from men.

In response to these persisting questions, I discuss some of the understandings about women's distinct positions revealed through the debate described as sameness versus difference, and the further contributions of poststructuralist theorizing. My concluding remarks refocus the questions away from an analysis of the problem to look instead at the answers that are always already present.

J.S. Frye identifies some of the significant issues in feminist literary criticism in her discussion of the tension between sameness and difference as represented by criticism found in Anglo-American and French feminist thinking. She succinctly describes the split in the debate between

> the dominant concern in American feminist criticism, with its experiential basis, and the dominant concern in much of French feminist criticism, as evident in the commitment and 'l'ecriture feminine' to language, theory, textual femininity, and the female unconscious. (1986, 15)

Although the experientially-based American feminist criticism is in danger of representing just one more sociological grouping, the French feminist insistence on speaking through the body renders women's difference to be essentialist, and nearly inaudible and inaccessible.

J.S. Frye names the sameness versus difference debate as the Scylla and Charybdis of feminist analysis (ibid., 15). The problem with such naming of sameness or difference, however, is that it assumes that to be different is to be apart from the standard, which in literature and the academic tradition is male. Schweickart (1986) suggests that, generally speaking, we remain captivated by the notion of maleness as the standard model of humanity.

Theories of difference and sameness are much more complicated than the polarity of meaning implied by the words. To say that women ascribe to one polarity or the other in their theory making is a denial of the consciousness that sees an issue as something beyond a single unitary position. The lack of resolution to this debate may be an indication that the question does not fit the evidence at hand; there is no generalization or single definition that will describe the multivocality of women's voices.

It should come as no surprise that voices which alternately claim positions of sameness or difference often sound contradictory, tentative, evasive, or impatient with each other. The challenge arises for feminists to use the tools of, and take positions within, a male-dominated construct such as the university without losing one's voice. The danger is that the feminist critique and knowledge, like women's knowledge in the past, may be reduced or simply conflated as another topic of discussion, reduced to sameness.

According to Culler, "feminist criticism . . . has had a greater effect on the literary canon than any other critical movement and . . . has arguably been one of the most powerful forces of renovation in contemporary criticism" (1982, 30). For some, feminist literary criticism is appealing because of the soundness and freshness of its argument, the reconnections between theory and life, and the re-examination of personal practice. Because of its appeal, it is possible to read and accept the analysis of feminist literary criticism and to ignore its political intent. Unless there is a connection between the theory and the political context of the cultural, such as in classroom practice, for example, feminist analysis will become another lifeless museum piece. An apt analogy made by Greta Nemiroff describes unacceptable one-way communication in women's studies classes as "talking head pedagogy" (1989, 3).

Feminist analysis that remains theoretical and propositional is a contradiction in terms. Divorce feminist literary analysis from its intent of social change and it becomes, with variations, much the same as any other literary theory. When the acceptance of feminist literary analysis amounts to no more than making room for a few more books on the library shelf, the distinct political intent has been dissolved in sameness. That is not to say there have been no changes at all in academia regarding the work of women. But no one should be too surprised or grateful that a few names of under-read women writers now appear on some reading lists. In spite of significant work of recovery and reinterpretation done by feminist theorists, the mainstream curricula shows little more than token recognition of women writers (Miller 1991).

The amount of reconceptualizing that takes place within a discipline in light of new theories is some indication of the seriousness with which the feminist theory is received. Miller notes that a recent job announcement at a major university called for a "feminist or theorist," implying that the categories are mutually exclusive. It appears that, as a body of knowledge that could influence the standard curriculum, feminist theory has yet to make a difference.

If, while teaching feminist theory, one accepts such obvious inequities as male-dominated reading lists and inequitable classroom practices which ignore the distribution of power between men and women, one is co-opting feminist analysis. Just as the adoption of gender equity programs does not necessarily promote feminist thought, it is possible to subvert the radical intent of feminist literary criticism by naming it as merely an alternative focus of discussion.

A "monologic" version of feminist literary theory, which implies there is one theory on which all feminists agree, obscures differences between women and removes differences based on race, class, and age. The assumption of sameness obscures individual variation, whereas the reification of difference fails to recognize any common ground shared by humanity.

In closing this section on women's knowledge, I want to acknowledge that "The Arbitrary Nature of Objectivity" section on theories of interpretation and representation is somewhat of an in-argument and will be unfamiliar to those not versed in literary theories. You may have noticed that I found it difficult to write this. You may be surprised to learn that this is the section I researched most heavily and for which I did the most reading. But still I can hear the critical voices in my head saying that I have got it wrong and that I must go back (where, I am not sure) until I get it "right." The experience is similar to the one in the seminar class mentioned in my journal in which I felt I did not know how to speak, that if only I had more expert knowledge I would have more authority. In the presence of critical voices, women either keep silent or speak in translation. Seeing nothing of myself reflected in places where I wanted to speak, I followed this pattern. It is this silencing before the experts which keeps things as they are. My experience in the seminar class galvanized my understanding of patriarchal organizations: no matter how knowledgeable, articulate, or compliant I became, the discourse was never intended for women to speak as women (Rich 1979). I had reached the limit of my private attempts to insert myself into the white, male system.

I was only able to write the previous section after reading the work of many women and men who speak of the constructedness of interpretation theory. I found the writing of feminist literary critics particularly inspiring as, although it was difficult at times, it made ideas accessible to me that I found exciting and full of hope. When in the midst of critical voices which would otherwise leave me silent, I relied heavily on my knowledge of other women's writing.

I have encountered women speaking and writing about the need for theories which reflect more of their complete and complex experience. The false split between objective/subjective evidence and public/private knowledge maintains a distinction between and a privileging of certain types of experience. The lie perpetuated by splitting these spheres militates against women's knowledge and experience of themselves as being capable of participating across these divisions. Women's lived experiences increasingly belie women's exclusion from the public realm; indeed, the interconnectedness of women's lives contradicts the assumptions about the actuality of such a split. Women writing as women subvert the division of their experience into polarities. Feminist theorizing of women's experience is subversive in its contradiction of the patriarchal organization of experience which attempts to ensure that the dichotomy remains viable.

The Difference of Language

Feminist literary criticism questions whether available language can elucidate women's lives, or whether women's use of language which is a male construct merely reinforces the status quo. Can women interpret their experience in any way other than how it is already interpreted through existing language? The experience itself is already an interpretation, and the reflection and articulation which follow are at least second- and thirdhand attempts to create meaning. A feminist commitment to participate in cultural change takes place in part through the reshaping of the conventions of language and form. The question raised by French feminist literary critics is that, if our language as an agent of change is suspect, how can language and its conventions be used to make transparent women's experience? What can be said for language-based media such as novels and classroom discourse if language and its use betray women?

In conversations with women about their classes, I often hear frustration expressed about their inability to participate and be heard as they would like. Unfortunately, some of the best intentions and the presumption of equal opportunity for male and female students only heighten their frustrations (Lewis and Simon 1986). This presumption of equality acts as an invisible barrier because, while it represents equal treatment of individuals, the male-dominated terms for approaching the material are clear and unequivocal. The difficulty of positioning one's theory in academic disciplines is mirrored in the attempts women students make to negotiate their physical space, language, and credibility in the classroom. For women students, the disjunction is most noticeable when they participate in all female sessions and alternately in mixed gender sessions. Regarding her experience of the latter, a friend of mine remarked, "I'm speaking a different language that they can't even hear." While I do not for a minute claim that women-exclusive sessions are unproblematic, the problems are compounded when women are not allowed to speak in their own voices; women, as a subdominant group, have learned to speak the language of domination and, for the most part, are relegated to speak their thoughts forever in translation.

Subdominant groups frequently bring the language of their private life into their public life, but it is not always heard. In educational institutions, the following also takes place.

Journal entry

> *Our class is taking a break. And what a class it has been—the women patient, silent, denying what they know, even to themselves. But now we have a break; just listen to them. Listen to the women, talking, talking, talking. There is something wrong here. During the class they think they are what is wrong.*
>
> *I have heard the women before. They are very bright. The questions they would ask are around, beside, and on top of the discussion. Their questions are critical, honest, engaged. The women are puzzled that they have so many questions. They think this means they are slow to catch on, that they don't understand, that they don't really belong here. These women think there is something wrong with the words they have used because the professor doesn't understand them.*

The journal entry depicts a scenario I have heard many times—women have to struggle to put their language into words that make sense to the instructors. Feminist students in particular frequently have to teach their supervisors something of a feminist perspective so that these faculty members can supervise them. Not surprisingly, the results are often unsatisfactory with the students being told that their feminist orientation is unacceptable.

The discussion of women's representation in texts is important because it finds women located neither in the ghetto of difference promoted by essentialism, nor as an addendum to the traditional canon, but as active agents in the creation of meaning. More than passive recipients of culture, women actively participate in the historical, specific, and contingent process in which their position is located. In this positioning women are both active and passive in the construction of society.

Like people unaccustomed to hearing their recorded voices, feminists theorize the sounds women's voices make, especially when they represent themselves in texts. Elaine Showalter asks "what is *the difference* of women's writing?" (1987, 248). We see that feminist literary criticism is more than what once was its principal mode: that of woman as reader. The emphasis is more strongly focused on gynocritics: women's writing, that is, "the study of woman as *writer*, of history, styles, themes, genres, and structures of writing by women; the psychodynamics of female creativity; the trajectory of the individual or collective female career; and the evolution and laws of a female literary tradition" (Schweickart 1986, 38). How is women's voice revealed? In the next section I discuss the location of women in both subjective and theoretical positions.

The "I" Witness Account

Chris Weedon asks, "how is one located in competing subjective realities and the social interests on behalf of which they work?" (1987, 8). I find this question significant as it provides some context for the admonition I mentioned earlier, that I be myself in a certain teaching situation. The admonition is difficult to carry out as I see that my "competing subjective realities" and "social interests" are more like a prism of fractured colours than a single white light.

This section has practical relevance to the question of how women will claim the right to speak about the texts and contexts which they read. Before they risk the exposure of their private voices made public, women will want to have considered these questions, which I first ask myself. As a student of literary theory, on what authority can I speak of what I know as a woman in a way that refuses the private/public split that I have learned too well? In acknowledgement of my gender, how will my words be received? In light of the views held by various theories of interpretation on the nature of womanness, where do I begin? And, as Gayatri Spivak asks, "who will listen?" (1990, 59)

Some of the answers begin by addressing the assumption that, in the feminist project to decentre the category "man," one cannot claim an essentialism for "woman." Humanist discourses offer a variety of essentialist explanations to describe the category "woman" as if she were a fixed, coherent subject (Weedon 1987). In contrast, a poststructuralist response suggests a decentred subjectivity in which there is no guarantee of meaning, subjectivity itself being an effect of discourse. This second response is not one that is easy for us as Western thinkers to understand and accept; I suspect that some of the difficulty lies in our desire for certainty in an explanation about how we come to be as we are. Our continual search for causes reflects our belief that one of the most important questions we can be asking is "why?" We also understand that the answer itself is not as important as our faith that indeed there is an answer. The poststructuralist decentred subjectivity is disturbing to those who return unfailingly to say, "yes, yes, I understand all that, but how are we gendered? How do we come to be essentially female or essentially male?" The poststructuralist response is that subjectivity and consciousness are socially produced in language and as such are a site of struggle and potential change (ibid., 41).

The attempt of various philosophies to describe the essential nature of human beings is outlined by Weedon. For example, liberal political philosophy assumes a unified rational consciousness; the belief that there is an essence of womanhood is at the heart of much radical-feminist discourse; and for the humanist Marxist, the true human nature is our champion against alienation by capitalism. Against these subjectivities, each of which is described as an irreducible human essence, "poststructuralism proposes a subjectivity which is precarious, contradictory and in process, constantly being reconstituted in discourse each time we think or speak" (ibid., 33).

Even though gender identity in psychoanalytic theory is not fixed to the same degree that it is in biological determinism, psychoanalysis assumes the existence of basic structures prior to their discursive realization (ibid., 50). A continual search for the origins of a gendered identity reflects our notion that meaning is given rather than constituted. It reflects our assumption, which we can hardly escape, that our humanness is fundamentally and essentially grounded. Regarding the designation of our sexuality, perhaps it is the same lack of certainty and determinism that society finds so disturbing, and that consequently prompts the call for virulent social control over how our sexuality is constituted in social relations.

The significance of abandoning this essential subjectivity of the human being is that it opens for discussion the forms that subjectivity may take. According to poststructuralists, the meaning of what it is to be a woman or man, for example, is produced historically and, as such, is open to change. These categories of man or woman are not immutable, but change with the range of discursive practices in which they are constituted. Weedon continues, "if we assume that subjectivity is discursively produced in social institutions and processes, there is no given reason why we should privilege sexual relations above other forms of social relation as constitutive of identity" (ibid., 50).

The qualities ascribed to one gender or another and the values we have attached to our practices are derived from social, changeable causes which do not rest on any inherently superior way of being. For example, a teacher who attempts to share power with students in a classroom can expect her or his efforts to be opposed and undervalued because, in general, the norm for interaction at universities has been inscribed as one-way from teacher to student and not co-operative or inclusive. Even though the dissimilar styles of sharing power versus wielding power could be judged as democratic versus authoritarian, respectively, the former will meet with less success because it is not what the institution, consisting of systems and people, has come to expect. We find it difficult to view actions as neutral if we already have an image of what we expect to see.

Weedon says that "social meanings are produced within social institutions and practices in which individuals, who are shaped by these institutions, are agents of change, rather than its authors, change which may either serve hegemonic interests or challenge existing power relations" (ibid., 25). Feminist use of poststructuralist theory demonstrates that if the power that supports a hegemonic system is neither fixed nor inherent in that system, then it is also available for use by those who are historically and materially constructed as powerless within the system.

The criticism of poststructuralism by feminist scholars such as Donovan is that in the pluralism and ambiguity of the decentred subject, the radical intent of the feminist project is neutralized. In other words, what is gone is not just a plurality of places for women to stand, but the very position of "woman." Deconstructionist theory blocks political identity and any kind of agency (1989, x-xi), thereby removing the grounding for a feminist politics. In that deconstructionism is described as "inherently anti-political and conservative" (ibid., xi), it parts company with feminist philosophy, despite sometimes running parallel to the latter's agenda. Jane Flax suggests that "the relation of feminist theorizing to the postmodern project of deconstructionism is necessarily ambivalent" (1990, 82). In the ambiguity that comes with the deferral of fixed meaning, feminist poststructuralism finds that the temporarily fixed meanings are located in historic and social discourse (Weedon 1987, 86). Since meaning has no external guarantee, the consequences of interpretation are, as I have suggested earlier, profoundly political.

The problem remains, then, how do we proceed as women to speak, write, and interpret our lives? Without a grounding in any field of inquiry or study but language, is women's writing abandoned to the invisible world of the non-living, waiting for attachment to and identity with one institution or another? It is not through relativism or the openness of liberalism that women presume to speak in their own voices. Access to agency in language occurs because, "by looking at a discourse *in operation*, in a specific historical context, it is possible to see whose interests it serves at a particular moment" (ibid., 111). Women's expression of themselves in text has the effect of constituting their experience as both object and subject of what they write and read. Insofar as women read and find written an argument for their own self-expression, women, both reader and writer, become the subject of the writing. This joint engagement of each other calls neutrality into question, and reading women's writing becomes a political act. In the feminist project, to come to terms with the historically mutable and changing forms of "woman," women claim power for self-definition, to speak themselves into the world.

J.S. Frye's explanation of "The Subversive 'I'" reveals how the novelistic form of first person singular—the "I am . . . is itself one of the most powerful expressions of women's capacity to resist cultural definition" (1986, 64). The one who calls herself "I" both defines herself and subverts entrapment as "other," as someone who is "different from," the standard (male) model of humanity. The character who sets in motion, interacts, and acts is always, already in motion, and is not a static reality acted upon by some authority or confined by some gender-specific definition. The narrating "I" claims selfhood, not in a static sense of a resemblance to other forms, but in a dynamic voice speaking with complexity and experience. "As the visible agent, the female 'I' refuses objectification and assumes the capacity to act" (ibid., 65). Margaret Atwood concludes, "the writer is both an eye-witness and an I-witness, the one to whom personal experience happens and the one who makes experience personal for others" (1982, 348).

Women are not adequately described by biologically-based theories of sexual difference or by scientific discourse as in Freudian theory. Neither are women to be identified by their specific social practices (Jacobus 1986) or rendered neutral by the abstract discourses of philosophy. The irony of the elusive representation of women in writing is that we assume the representation is there at all, that the struggle for self-definition remains even though the definition is repressed and identified as "other." Whether reflected in women's literary tradition, language, or culture, the search for this representation is, according to Jacobus, a political response. She writes:

> the emphasis on women's writing politicizes in a flagrant and polemical fashion the "difference" which has traditionally been elided by criticism and by the canon formations of literary history. To label a text as that of a woman, and to write about it for that reason, makes vividly legible what the critical institution has either ignored or acknowledged only under the sign of inferiority. We need the term "women's writing" if only to remind us of the social conditions under which women wrote and still write—to remind us that the conditions of their (re)production are the economic and educational disadvantages, the sexual and material organizations of society, which, rather than biology, form the crucial determinants of women's writing. (ibid., 63-64)

Waiting for the arrival of the "most correct" reason for being able to speak at all will, of course, continue women's silence. The search for such an answer holds two assumptions which tie in to the rationalist, essentialist thinking which we find so hard to avoid. First, the assumption that there is a "correct" feminism, or even women's standpoint has, already been soundly laid aside by other writers as the appeal for one essentialism over another. Second, it is harder to begin without answers to essentialist questions if we still believe in the efficacy of such questions to validate our acts. In the meantime, whether women are feminists or have ever read a word of any philosophy (which excludes more than it includes), the power relations in their lives are carried out in material conditions of contest and struggle. It is not necessary to have a particular ideological orientation to know you are oppressed, discounted, marginalized. Perhaps the refusal to accept these conditions is a pre-condition for self-definition and speech. It is in the local, historical, and contingently-constructed discourse that women act as agents on their own behalf and in concert with others in the production of meaning.

The project of gynocritics, as defined by Elaine Showalter, encompasses the notion that criticism alone does not establish women's voices. For her the focus on reading as women has long passed and the issue at hand is the sound of women's voices in their writing. Freedom from essentialism and the determination of the subject encourage and challenge women to uncover their own complicity with domination and to discover what it means not only to reproduce their history, but to do so in ways that affirm their present.

CHAPTER FOUR

The University as (Con)text

JOURNAL ENTRY

This is not the first time I have experienced this unsettling mixture of self-doubt, anger, and confusion. For the class today, I had done the readings diligently. Sometimes I didn't understand them, but pushed on because I want to learn what people think and say about topics like language and learning, hermeneutics, and the dialectic. I had done my homework, made notes, had several questions to ask and opinions to offer on some of them. I was prepared. But I left anyway. The feeling I had today as I walked downtown across the bridge was not unlike what I remember feeling when I was a child, when my brother and his friends ran away when they saw me coming, and my mother told me that girls don't play boys' games.

I learned a lot from today. I am quite astounded at the gripping quality—perhaps prehensile—of my fear of being wrong. It was partly a set-up too—here where I want so desperately to be right. I am not berating myself for not speaking up because if I had been able to speak I would have done so. As well, it is futile for me to make this class a private crusade to revamp every class I take so that it offers students, particularly women, more than just an "objective" discourse. But how does anyone circumvent this academic hegemony and learn to speak, for example, using the personal narrative? Whatever has to happen, I have quite a long way to go in affirming my own voice before speaking in front of potential critics.

Some of the conclusions my mind would like to draw, right or

> *not, are these: (1) I need to learn more about the topic under discussion so I will have the confidence to speak up. (2) I should just stop trying to participate in these classes because there are other things I can do anyway. (3) I will go back and make myself speak in a way that is useful to me. (4) I need to practise making conscious what I know so that I can articulate it to the class. (5) I am interested in the wrong topic. (6) The male right to define knowledge is men's power over women.*
>
> *I won't forget how I was silenced today because, by losing my voice, I somehow have developed clearer vision. I know I'm going to find something worthwhile to do with my insight and anger.*

Commentary

My experience in the seminar class is, in many ways, marked by its ordinariness and routine pattern. Some might wonder what kind of privileged life I must have led until that time if the class I have described qualified as a traumatic experience. But, as a result I realized that up until then, my privilege as a white woman had permitted me to negotiate, compromise, and privately arrange to feel included in the Western, androcentric, heterosexist discourse. I was angry that my training in this discourse made it difficult even then to imagine seriously what else had been left out. I came to see that the feminist struggle at the academy is not about being accepted or legitimated by those in authority, but, as Adrian Rich (1979) says, it is about claiming one's education and indeed one's personhood, too.

It is clear that the Western, masculinist hegemony over the daily life of the academy has a vested interest in the status quo. Of the many sites from which to begin addressing the need for systemic change, most appealing to me is the congruence between rhetoric and practice espoused by feminist pedagogy.

Another Introduction

In the previous chapters I have been describing the setting in which the practices of feminist pedagogy daily contest for the hearts and minds of women and men in the promotion of structural and social change and equality. By locating the discussion of feminist pedagogy in increasingly specific historical and material practices of the university, I have metaphorically placed the discussion in concentric circles that move, like a reverse wave, from the outside in.

The first and outermost circle describes the university setting and its receptiveness to a feminist agenda given the quest for certainties and the demands for truth. How and what knowledge is interpreted and reported depends largely on the methodology of choice, and consequently there is much formal and informal control over the politics of methodology. Within the university context, a second circle examines the arbitrariness of specific disciplinary criteria and the consequent struggle for people on the periphery to find self-definition and voice. Women and other marginalized people argue for a recognition at the disciplinary level of their construction of knowledge. The third circle looks at the practices called feminist pedagogy and at the students and teachers who set the practices in motion.

What is Feminist Pedagogy?

The feminist pedagogical process is difficult to name even when those doing the naming can specify precisely what they want to see as an outcome or goal. There is no single best picture of what it looks like either in its representation or methods, or in its aims. The difficulty of naming a feminist pedagogy increases when we acknowledge the plurality of women's voices, feminist theories, points of view, and political agendas. Every text on pedagogy I read adds yet another question to the series of questions already asked. What does feminist pedagogy look like? How does it happen? Why does it not happen more often?

There are those who look for facile solutions to these questions and who ask feminist teachers for categorical descriptions of their pedagogy compared to "regular" teaching or critical educational practices. Many who ask have not taken seriously or have never understood the dilemma facing women in positions of authority who struggle not to reproduce oppressive conditions for others.

I have avoided answering these questions for three chapters by first addressing the context in which feminist pedagogy may be applied. I have outlined some of the reasons why feminist practices are not welcomed, if indeed they are tolerated. For, in addition to challenging the university discourse in terms of what qualifies as knowledge, how knowledge is constructed, and whether it reflects women's experiences, feminist critical pedagogy also addresses the social context of education and the relations and power of particular interests.

The examples of teaching strategies provided by people who have taught from a feminist perspective are marked as much by their diversity as by their agreement—carried out in endless variations—on the need for social change in women's lives. Diverse strategies are surely required given the oppression under which women suffer and the stratifications, such as race, age, and sexual orientation, which are as inseparable from each of us as is our gender.

There is no prescription or recipe for how to carry out this activity that I, for the sake of convenience, call feminist pedagogy. As a distinct body of knowledge about educational practices, feminist pedagogy does not exist. While it is not difficult to describe some of the forms that have become familiar in many feminist classes, a description of these forms should not be mistaken for a description of feminist pedagogy. Classes which are learner-centred, discussion-based, consensus-forming, interactive, self-disclosing, and creative are also part of many adult education programs which are based on humanistic learning principles. While use of one or more of these forms may create the possibility of a feminist pedagogy, they do not define how this interpretive and creative process takes place. The lack of specificity does not come simply from the relative newness of interest in feminist practices or in their inordinate scope. Rather, the teaching event, as an interpretive process, cannot be discussed separately from the context of the classroom, including the power relations, from the politics of the topic, or from the people involved.

The discussion that follows is not an attempt to acknowledge a correct theory or correct form of practice, but to acknowledge that feminist practice is "not an empirically knowable entity but lies in ways of thinking" (Probyn 1990, 178). What I am discussing is not so much a set of practices as an attitude, an understanding or personal belief about the commitment to feminist agendas for social change. Feminist pedagogy is, more than anything else, a political act for social change in the conditions of women's lives.

Is the Subject Fixed Yet?

The feminist poststructuralist view that I discussed in the last section of Chapter 3 helps to elucidate what I mean by a feminist pedagogy. In the departure from the poststructuralism of Lacan, Barthes and others, feminist poststructuralism assumes a subjectivity in order "to make sense of society and ourselves" (Weedon 1987, 173). The significance of this assumption of women's subjectivity is that it is played out in the absence of universal notions about truth, essential humanism, and the prescriptions of gender. Instead, women's subjectivity is located in the particular material conditions, the discursive practices, and the everydayness of women's experiences. As educators we can ask ourselves what modes of subjectivity are open for us to read and what are the implications in political terms. Not surprisingly, the university system is also founded in "conditions of existence which are at one and the same time both material and discursive" (ibid., 8). In this reading, classroom practices of power and discourse are a necessary part of what is examined in feminist pedagogy. The particular ways of fixing identity and meaning are important to recognize for their political implications for both students and teachers.

Feminist political practice is "a patchwork of overlapping alliances" spoken of "in the plural as the practice of feminisms" (Nicholson 1990, 35). This plurality recognizes that, even though we cannot ever come to know each other as fully as we describe ourselves, we can decide to act together in ways that defend the differences that will never be shared. It may be presumptuous to assume we have a complete understanding of even our own personal practices in a society in which we are never fully aware of the extent to which conscious practices such as patriarchy are also constructed in the unconscious. Feminist postructuralism recognizes that knowledge of present experience is not given, but constructed, and that knowledge, the Other, and we ourselves are locally and contingently constituted.

Within the feminist political agenda, practice is attentive to more than the theoretical prerequisites of dealing with diversity; it is a pedagogy that also takes seriously the reality of the Other in practical terms. The contradicting and shifting positions of all classroom participants requires an examination of how notions of liberating practice and empowerment will be contested by both teachers and learners. The paragraphs that follow illustrate some of the ways diversity is recognized in an atmosphere in which change for all parties can take place.

Elizabeth Ellsworth's excellent article (1989) describes her experiences as a white middle-aged woman and professor engaged with students in developing an anti-racist course. Many writers have found that her experience is common to issues in feminist pedagogy, particularly the sources of tension in a classroom that come from the power residing in each participant's subject position. How will participants speak to each other across differences of gender, race, age, orientation, institutional authority, and many other distinct positions? Calls for a collective liberation or for resistance to oppression easily mask the particular experiences and backgrounds of participants. Ellsworth's article raises other questions shared by feminist pedagogy: what diversity do we silence in the name of "liberatory" education? Or, how can feminist pedagogy avoid strategies which repress differences such as race, class, age (to name but a few)? And, what is required of the teacher and students?

Students in Ellsworth's class noted that in the discourse of some other anti-racist classes, certain groups ended up oppressing women and adopting an analysis that excluded students of some ethnicities. In the midst of tension produced by their differences, students in these classes learned that their struggle against racism came not only from their common commitment, but also from what they did not share—their gender, sexual orientation, ethnicity, and other differences. Each person had a particular view of racism based on his or her personal experience and on the social history of the distinct group to which each person belonged. As part of larger groups elsewhere, their strategies for fighting racism had to be interrogated for the implications that the strategies had for recreating an oppression in another sphere. In other words, how could their anti-racist strategies make things better without making them worse? The students' proposed interrogation of strategies asked: "to what extent do our political strategies and alternative narratives about social difference succeed in alleviating campus racism while at the same time managing *not to undercut* the efforts of other social groups to win self-definition?" (ibid., 318). For students, conditions of oppression were not abstract, but particular and rooted not only in their own experience, but in the experience of the group of which they were part. Discussions of anti-racist strategies could happen only by being informed of the various subject positions of other students as well as the teacher.

The questions of identity, representation, and action raised in Ellsworth's classroom are similar to the ones I noted earlier raised by women writers who claim space to write of their own identity within their contradictory position in patriarchy. The process of claiming one's subject position, however contradictory and shifting, is informed by communication with and parallel efforts in other quarters such as feminist literary theory, feminist pedagogy, anti-racist pedagogy, and feminist research methodology. These practices and others struggle with what it means to function with the shifts in power that come with having varied subject positions, such as alternately being both privileged and oppressed. The academic women are privileged by virtue of their relative positions within elite educational institutions. However, in that the institutions remain dominated by masculinist, Western thought and action, women's subject position is never unproblematic.

Methodology as Pedagogical Matrix

A paper by Kate Sandilands on feminist research, draws many conclusions that are equally applicable to concerns around pedagogical practices. In a way that is useful for education, she defines method as part of the social construction of reality and as the practice of knowledge. Her following remarks about research apply equally well to the discussion of how pedagogy may be carried out.

> The point is not . . . to use feminist research to validate any and all frames of reference. Rather, if our goal is to use knowledge (of

> the self and the world) to effect change, then we are capable of using the tension between statuses, between "insider" and "outsider," to build a set of partial affinities, a coalition of related and critically self-reflective interests rather than a totalizing strategy of unidimensionally defined identifications. These processes can and do begin in the particular situations of feminist research, and constitute our chosen method of understanding. (1990, 18)

In like manner, there is no single feminist pedagogy because there is no single representation of identity or reality as "our knowledge of the particular is derived from both theoretical and contextual insight" (ibid.). The living out of feminist theory within the context of patriarchal institutions is, perhaps, the greatest challenge to feminist pedagogy.

In a discussion of research methods, Sandilands states that the problem of the researcher dominating the researched cannot be overcome simply by allowing the participant to define her or his own agenda and to speak her or his own life without interruption. The same dilemma exists for a teacher who does not wish to dominate a women's studies class by having students reach some sense of empowerment through consciousness raising understood in the teacher's framework. More specifically, what does the teacher do with her own knowledge and agenda in light of students' experience?

The difference in power cannot be erased by the use of empathy which, in fact, may exacerbate the domination. The expression of empathy has the potential to detract from or subsume the subject positions identified by race, class, or sexuality (or nationality, region, time, age). The empathic expression "I understand" sets up the structure wherein all differences between the two are measured against the definition of "how am I the same?" (ibid., 17). How identity is maintained in the classroom is a question raised by the liberal humanist and the critical pedagogue alike. In light of the subjugation of women's knowledge, feminist pedagogy is especially sensitive to the voice of the non-dominant discourse, the voice of the Other. Feminist theory and classroom practice work against a situation in which the discourse remains grounded in the teacher's version of identity, "which will, in that context, define the truth of the situation" (ibid.).

Feminist theory is informed by first-person accounts which provide information and expand available knowledge. Perhaps what is even more important is that the strength of the first-person accounts which form the basis of an understanding, underscores women's interpretations of themselves and the world. Whether the outcome is intended or not, women's critical interpretations of their social positions are a form of political practice and consciousness raising. The success of this political practice that is much at odds with traditional academic discourse has earned consciousness raising a bad name in academic circles. For women and other subordinate groups, however, the practice of coming to know is seen as an act of insubordination. This insistence on the personal or at least the positional is at odds with institutionalized meanings that privilege patriarchy as a universal interpretation.

Misreading Feminist Pedagogy

Tension arises due to the gap between feminist theoretical knowledge and the institutional practices which are permitted for reaching an understanding of this knowledge. This gap between theory and practice is the difficulty or pitfall inherent in critical pedagogy, the ideas of which, in many ways, are not dissimilar to those of feminist pedagogy. Some of the terms used in critical pedagogy, however, such as "empowerment," "student voice," "dialogue" and "critical reflection" need further examination to see that, as noted by Ellsworth (1989), they are not actually repressive myths. For example, for whose empowerment is this model at work? Who will do the empowering, and to what end? A system that assumes fully rationalized, individual subjects capable of agreeing on universalizable principles is, by virtue of its assumptions, incapable of uncovering the patriarchal structures of power and knowledge and other organizing bases in the classroom; the conscious and unconscious processes of both students and teachers remain equally opaque. Rationality as a tool of critical discourse has a way of silencing those whose notion of empowerment does not match that offered by the instructor. Students and the instructor arrive in the classroom in an unequal power relationship that rationality, even if it can name the differences, cannot effectively alter.

If the assumptions, goals, and issues concerning who produces knowledge remain untheorized and unaddressed, "critical pedagogues will continue to perpetuate relations of domination in their classrooms" (ibid., 297). Ellsworth observes that the discourse of critical pedagogy, by reproducing relations of domination in the classroom, has itself become a vehicle of oppression. The idea of who the students "should" be and what "should" be happening in the classroom ignores the specificity of the classroom content and the social identities of the individuals who comprise the class.

Critical pedagogy has a way of satisfying itself with its own theory, a way of relying on the power of discourse to come to an understanding of the Other. But merely setting up the ground rules for dialogue does not address the various forms of resistance to participation, or the need for acknowledgement of how one is implicated in the information. The writing of Henry Giroux, for example, misses the point about resistance. In formulaic fashion he envisages that, in the goals of dialogue, all voices will be unified in their identification of suffering and their desire to alleviate it (1988, 72). Unfortunately, the assumption that dialogue will undo the asymmetrical positions of difference and privilege does not make it so. Such assumptions about the fairness of the democratic process can make it even more difficult for the non-dominant to speak. Assumptions about the unity of efforts and values conflates differences in a way that is repressive as it aligns participants into "us" and "them" status. In a classroom, attempts to achieve a harmony of interests may be both impossible and undesirable if the rules of dialogue are used as yet another way to manipulate the range of interpretations. Gayatri Spivak, quoted in Ellsworth (1989, 322), calls the search for a coherent narrative "counterproductive." In Ellsworth's anti-racist class, the collective struggle was not made on the basis of sameness, but on the acknowledgement that unity was fragmentary and unstable; not given, but chosen.

I think it is a simple matter for the radical intent of feminist pedagogy to be left out, leaving an approach which resembles critical pedagogy. When this elision occurs, feminist pedagogy loses its radicalness and begins to look like nothing more than many other classroom situations characterized by student discussion, sometimes heated, around a particular social issue. In Ellsworth's classroom, it was not enough to make oppression relative by claiming it as the one thing all students had in common; rather, it became necessary to clarify the oppression and insist that it be understood and struggled against contextually. The task was seen "not as one of building democratic dialogue between free and equal individuals, but building a coalition among the multiple, shifting, intersecting and sometimes contradictory groups carrying equal weights of legitimacy within the culture and the classroom" (ibid., 317).

Feminist pedagogy is ripe for co-optation into other pedagogical forms because, for one thing, it is difficult to do and sustain given the uncertainty of what can be known and what should be done. As well, the position of the teacher is neither prescribed nor predicted in any theoretical framework of classroom methodology. In the reformulation of pedagogy and knowledge, feminist practice is profoundly contextual and interdependent.

The richness of feminist pedagogy stems from an explicit recognition of a "plurality of understandings, [a] rejection of a single 'truth for all women'"(Sandilands 1990, 19). At the same time, this richness also makes it difficult to resist co-optation or lapsing of such a generous philosophy into a liberal notion of individuality. The feminist political agenda of social change, however, serves as the main criterion by which feminist pedagogues can decide whether they are making their practice better without making it worse. In other words, can they avoid adding to the oppression or silencing that some students already experience? A quotation from Sandilands summarizes this positioning.

> We speak, then, from both specificity and context relevant generality; what we speak are not immutable truths upon which we reflect and act. They are not, I suggest, mere "opinion," but are self-critical and contextual statements of purposively-constructed generality which, to paraphrase Engels, are "valid" insofar as they are applicable in practice. (ibid., 12)

But how are we to assess what is valid and applicable in practice? While some assessments can only be made while the action is taking place, we can also use theoretical knowledge to predict what some outcomes will likely be. What will feminist pedagogical theory come to mean when it is put into practice? An example follows in which I use feminist theory to examine suggestions for a certain set of practices.

Judging by the plethora of self-help books offering theories and/or practices of how to make sense of the world, the search for meaning in people's lives is being conducted at a scavenger hunt pitch. We see popular evidence of the desire to understand the changes in female/male relations brought about since the women's movement in the 1960s and 1970s. Books with theories about how gender relations work (or do not work), followed by solutions, are found in nearly every bookstore. Let us consider as an example, the outcomes of the solutions proposed by popular writer Anne Wilson Schaef (Schaef and Fassel 1988). In order to assess its usefulness in women's lives, I will follow one of Schaef's most popular theories to draw some conclusions about its practical applications. In *Women's Reality*, Schaef describes what she calls the White Male System as a world view in which power and influence are held by males and perpetuated by them (1982, 7). This system is one in which we all participate. Schaef uses addictions theory research to describe the similarities between the White Male System and substance or process addictions. She says that it is most important to look at how we react to the White Male System because, just as co-dependent behaviour on the part of others actively perpetuates the process of the addict, certain reactive behaviour, particularly on the part of women, also perpetuates the actions of those who operate according to the White Male System. Schaef's most remarkable claim is that if people stopped living in what she calls the Reactive Female System, then the White Male System would collapse.

She suggests that there are alternate processes that are supportive and life giving that do not work to perpetuate the White Male System. Rather than being inextricably tied to a malignant process in the way co-dependency and addictions are linked, Schaef's theory offers alternative choices for feminist action beyond this unhealthy dualism. Schaef's addictions theory, unlike many others, focuses on a systemic addiction as opposed to a single behaviour or substance. I will assess her theory—as one which enjoys some popularity among women—in relation to the potential for the promotion of social change for women.

First, in addictions theory generally, the co-dependent is restored to wholeness by refocusing attention from the problems of the addict to the needs of the co-dependent. Similarly, as demonstrated by the focus of the previous chapter, feminist literary criticism is not concerned so much with a critique of the androcentrism of the canon, but with gynocritics, and the development of women's aesthetic and forms of writing. Women's agenda and literary production exists without comparison to the white male canon as the standard for knowing. Feminist pedagogical practices and women's knowledge about themselves are their own referents for knowledge claims. Schaef would agree that a feminist agenda is not centred on revealing the shortcomings or correcting the partial knowledge of men's studies.

However, Schaef's recommendations, like other addictions theory writing, implies a cause and effect relationship, albeit a complex one, between the system of patriarchy and its victims. Two problems which follow from this indicate how the effect of patriarchy is both overestimated and underestimated in women's lives. Using addiction theory, the role assigned to women as co-dependents once again leaves women in the position of victim. Schaef's claim that co-dependence is what keeps the addictive system in place leaves the responsibility for change with the victim herself. Further, the victim has no alternative but to blame herself when this conversion has not yet been accomplished. The problem is that this analysis ends up blaming the victim and making her responsible for the solutions. In the face of such analysis, we need to ask if this works toward social change and whether women's interests are served by continually holding women responsible for the injustice done to them.

Whereas patriarchy may colour large portions of women's lives, women also find agency to act out their lives in ways that are not simply responses to patriarchal hegemony. Women also interact with other forces, both supportive and non-supportive, as co-determinants in their lives. The interface with patriarchy is not its victim's entire life.

There is a second response to Schaef's admonition that patriarchy will end if its victims stop supporting it. Evidence of patriarchy, as well as being concrete and visible, is also manifest in victims' lives in ways that are not easily recovered or amenable to behaviour modification. Behavioural change on the part of victims, which means assuming the role of non-victim, is a kind of "bootstrapism" that hides the systemic nature of the problem. It does not encourage the kind of self-reflection needed to see patriarchy as it constructs Western political thought and action.

The question of the correct theories and concomitant practices is always a dilemma in the midst of complex social relations. I believe that while there is never a single right answer, there are several ways in which the best of intentions will be compromised in practice. For example, in commenting on the use of deconstructionism in much of American literary criticism, Weedon notes that a large proportion of deconstructive textual analysis reaffirms the status quo. "The implicit assumption that there is a free play of meaning not already located in a hierarchical network of discursive relations is to deny social power by rendering it invisible" (1987, 165).

Feminist practices illustrate that it is discourse which helps to name the social and material conditions of our existence and permits discussion of how the conditions oppress us. As stated earlier, however, discourse does not necessarily bring to light the conditions of our oppression that are unconscious. Discourse and the ideas of a critical pedagogy, for example, are useful up to a point, but in the end, they do not go far enough to provide a motive for action. Critical pedagogy clouds the fact that it is not moving forward in terms of alleviating problems of social context, particular interests, and power, particularly regarding the gendered identity that students negotiate in their everyday lives. For women students, there is both a desire to know and an upsetting of existing power relations. Men students also experience a threat to the basis of their power in society (Lewis 1990). Feminist pedagogy is more than a critical analysis; it acknowledges and provides for the fact that a feminist critique can be dangerous for women. Feminist pedagogy needs to "address the threat to women's survival and livelihood that a critique of patriarchy in its varied manifestations confronts" (ibid., 473).

The issue remains that, while there are many ways in which feminist theory and practice can be sidelined and co-opted without changing the status quo, the inverse corollary is equally dangerous: that we take no action out of fear of co-optation. In an effort to have the right theory and action, we can become immobilized. In examining the result of any actions, we can be made to feel that what we do is never enough, never completely correct, or worse, that it might be co-opted and used against its original purpose (Price 1988). For example, one might wonder how academic feminists who work to transform practice can be providing anything more than an educational institutionalized fix by teaching at an institution that is in many ways antithetical to their commitment as feminists. Or, how may a discussion of feminist pedagogy be more preoccupied by words and less concerned with practice?

The fear of co-optation and the desire for solidarity against outside criticism can lead women's groups to work with a narrow range of acceptable theory and practice. Feminist groups often generate borders and dichotomies in the desire for unity or wholeness against the alienation and individualism of society. Young suggests "that the desire for mutual understanding and reciprocity underlying the ideal of community is similar to the desire for identification that underlies racial and ethnic chauvinism" (Young 1990, 311). Unfortunately, when women can speak only about those issues on which there is agreement, the desire for community helps to reproduce homogeneity. Factionalism and the inability to understand the Other while professing similar ideologies comes as a disappointment for those hoping for solidarity and congruent action. The ideal of community, however, fails to address the political question of face-to-face relations (ibid., 302). In other words, how can we be transparent to or claim understanding of another when our understanding of ourselves is partial and contingent at best? I think that the expectation of community and the desire for affirmation and support from like-minded people is a luxury we cannot expect when deciding to take action with others. Coalitions for single project purposes acknowledge that the remainder of the participating groups' agendas could potentially be incompatible with one another.

The cultural assumption that community is the opposite of individualism is similar to the assumption that femininity and masculinity are opposites. The lack of congruence with this assumption leaves the impression that, if the like-mindedness promised in community has failed, then the project has failed. Some understandings of community do include the politics of difference of which Young speaks. She concludes that

> . . . the concept of social relations that embody openness to unassimilated otherness with justice and appreciation needs to be developed. Radical politics, moreover, must develop discourse and institutions for bringing differently identified groups together without suppressing or subsuming the differences. (ibid., 320)

In the feminist project, it is the naming of oppression in the historical, the local, and the particular which grounds deliberate action and provides motivation for choosing to work with others.

This acceptance of differences is a great challenge to feminist practice partly because of the desire to protect feminist interests from outsiders and from criticism. But it is the lure of a right theory and essentialist, monologic thinking that would seduce feminist practice into an ever closer fit with traditional institutions. As part of its acceptance into the academy, feminist practice is encouraged to provide grand metanarratives to explain the loose ends, to make things clear so that everyone will finally be able to understand what feminism is all about. Feminist pedagogy is made more difficult by assumptions such as these and by the expectations routinely placed on critical discourse, consensus, group affiliation, and community.

What Do We Do On Monday?

Even though one of the strengths of feminism is its ability to engage in many struggles simultaneously and to permit contradictory understandings, the contested terrain is classroom practice. Practical constraints always intrude in any efforts to speak openly about differences of opinion and experiences (Sandilands 1990, 18). In the reality of the classroom, how much contextual insight will be permitted by the students, the teacher, or the institution?

The need for feminist pedagogy in institutions like the university is so great that it would be a luxury to wait for the correct theoretical stance before taking action. The promotion of women's issues has so many agenda items worthy of immediate action that, if it were possible, everything, everywhere, would need to be begun at once. While the discussions of pedagogical theory may be illuminating and perhaps find some agreement with the reader's thinking, it is in the classroom that theories and contextual insights are put to the test.

Feminist understandings of partial and subjugated knowledges are at odds with a teaching institution in which students have come to expect nothing more than overarching theories and "proven facts." Demands of some students for "right answers" lead many teachers to approach the concept of knowledge as nothing more than a marketable commodity.

A problem with describing teaching practices that are compatible with the feminist intent of social change through political action is that, while the theory is acceptable as theory at the university, the teaching practices which are implicit in the theory cannot so readily find a place. Indeterminacy, contingency, and the local construction of knowledge are not so easily accommodated by institutions concerned with systems and accountability and quantitative evaluation. Besides teaching feminist theory as a subject, however, teachers address the needs that will permit them to examine these sites of struggles and contradictions. The experience of Magda Lewis is instructive.

Lewis talks about the difficulty of encouraging women students to reread or reconsider their subject positions that have given them their compromised status within patriarchy. Women students need to know that there is both knowledge and emotional support for the time when they willingly expose their experiences of inequality and violation. Public and private rereading of one's position within patriarchy is both a liberation and a threat, a threat that is "used as justification for continued violation" (1990, 477). In her pedagogical practices, Lewis emphasizes women students' participation in their right to create meaning for themselves as a step beyond their demand that they have the right to do so.

Women understand that their efforts to create new emotional and concrete space for themselves requires courage and support. They have seen the violence that attends their words and actions when, consciously or not, they contradict their patriarchal roles. Feminist pedagogical practices are indeed a threat to existing power relations in which students find themselves. Women have seen that they do not even have to be a feminist to encounter overt violence in an academic setting, to which the death of women students at the Université de Montréal attests. Lewis concludes, "we must choose words carefully and negotiate analysis with the women students in ways that will not turn them away from the knowledge they carry in their experiences" (ibid., 474).

Many feminists have written about their teaching experiences that enabled women to self-consciously address their own meaning-making. The discussion that follows is about particular practices that worked for feminist instructors in their classrooms. I present the practices as they are described in the literature without any attempt to group them into categories or to generalize about them.

1) Michele Russell begins the educative process in the present material conditions of the classroom itself (1985, 163). Instead of dealing in abstractions, she exhorts us to "use everything." She describes the way in which the small and unyielding classroom furniture made the ample-bodied, mostly Black students feel awkward, restless, and furtive. Russell starts with the physical conditions of the classroom to discuss the unnecessary ways in which the educational process makes people feel slighted and uncomfortable. Russell's "use of everything" makes problematic "what is" in an examination of the education activity.
2) Janice Raymond calls on feminists to teach passionately, not by preaching or proselytizing, but by being unguarded in showing that

we care about learning. Passion is involved in showing students the proud traditions of women and in teaching students that we think they are capable of doing the same. Feminist teaching is not a disembodied enterprise. "We look at our subject with passion because we are our subject" (1985, 58).

3) Barbara Hillyer Davis (1985) describes the difficulty of educating students who possess varying abilities in feminist analysis. Traditional students need to learn how to analyze their lives as women, while the "advanced" students need to learn to appreciate the life stories of women and men who struggle with traditional perspectives. Segregating the groups into "beginning" and "advanced" may be an easy solution, but it is not a good one. The difficulty in educating both new and seasoned learners in the presence of the others is largely a problem of language. By interacting with each other, the beginning groups learn the words, ideas, and language of feminist discourse and the advanced groups act as translators, observing in others the power of language to change consciousness.
4) Margo Culley believes that the details and injustices in women's lives are cause for anger, a force which she investigates with her classes on women's issues. Her goal is "to permit the acknowledgement and claiming of anger as one's own, and to direct its legitimate energy toward personal and social change" (1985, 212). She begins her large lecture classes of 250 students with readily available, public statistics on the facts of women's lives concerning education, employment, and income levels. Students are often startled and angered by the data and soon begin challenging the sources, validity, and method of compiling the data, as well as questioning the professor's relationship to men. She examines the issues with the students and looks at the anger in a lesson on the displacement of negative feelings. In acknowledging their anger, she asks the students to consider the anger in society directed towards women. She asks them why "the culture allows overt and often violent hatred of women, but does not permit, indeed has no word for, anger at men?" (ibid., 213). She concludes that feminist teachers cannot expect students to experience anger if we will not acknowledge that we ourselves are so moved.
5) Charlotte Bunch (1983) advises us that feminist teaching should include the development of feminist theory. By means of theory, women can come to understand the forces that work against them and those who are engaged in day-to-day political activity can use theory to develop visions which sustain their activism. Theory grows out of activism and reflection; it acts as a guide for sorting out options and keeps us from becoming overwhelmed and immoblilized.

Bunch teaches students how to develop theory by dividing the process into four interrelated parts. The first step is to describe what exists—a process of interpreting and naming the reality of the conditions of women's lives. Second is the analysis of why that reality exists, being careful to avoid explaining everything all at once with a single concept. The third part is the vision of what should exist, a process which enables students to assess actions in light of long- and short-term goals. Last is the formulating of strategies for promoting change; this includes drawing out the consequences of theory.

Women see that doing theory is not "too hard" or beyond them when the theory formation begins with the conditions of their lives and an examination of assumptions they make daily about their being in the world. The women practise their theory making skills in exercises that help them think creatively. From their own experiences, they see that there is not a "correct line" as in the political sense, or a "correct answer" as in academia.

6) Some of the most innovative teaching comes from classes and schools organized outside traditional institutions which often find feminists too radical for existing modes of pedagogy (Hammer 1983, 219). As an extra-institutional event, Barbara Hammer taught film-making by holding classes in her own studio. Women learned how to create images of themselves that were a reflection of their own politics. Teaching in a non-traditional setting reduced anxiety and permitted women to explore and receive acknowledgement for their total effort and not just the part targetted for evaluation. Women envisioned the scope for their possibilities well beyond the limitations of the institutional evaluative process.

7) The Women's School of Planning and Architecture (Weisman and Birkby 1983) grew from the convictions of architects, planners, and teachers who found their common interests and goals not being met within existing architecture and planning institutions. The establishment of their school reflected the organizers' feminist beliefs that, in all aspects, the design process could be organized as if women mattered. They concluded that feminist education could not occur in any place that did not also include women's politics, creative talents, or life works. In their evolving consciousness and practice, they identified the most important factors in feminist education as theory, feminist analysis, and ideology, as well as a context and practical demonstration of those values. They conclude that, unlike analysis, a feminist education cannot take place in traditional academic institutions unless feminist values are also reflected through changes in behaviour and action.

This discussion of feminist pedagogy does not end in a definitive statement of what this pedagogy is which promotes a feminist interpretation of texts. Such a pedagogy can at best be identified as an elucidation of foundational thought, broadly stated, with a clear understanding that what is at stake is the uncovering of meaning in women's lived experiences. The philosophy may reach some conclusions and name some practices, but a description of feminist pedagogy like the guiding principles for an adequate feminist politics, "cannot be specified in advance since the precise configuration of power relations in any situation will determine how best we can act" (Weedon 1987, 11).

The reductionism of natural science that feminist research methodology resists is just as unhelpful as the grand totalizing theories of education that try to address all issues for all people, for all time. One absolute is as misleading as another. Therefore feminist pedagogy cannot be a prescription. The advancement of feminist interpretation of theory and practice is obtained by contingency and balance which offer little security and require great courage. Any description of feminist practices simply outlines some things that worked for some people in their classes. What is written here is intended to be information that will help us read with more understanding the text that is the university, the subject discipline, each other, and ourselves.

Concluding Remarks

I have discussed the representation of women as writers and as interpreters of their experience in the university context. In general, one of the predominant concerns in feminist literary criticism is the capacity of literature to represent women's experiences, given the consequences of male encoding. The concern about women's representation in literature is a concrete issue in the defining of a feminist hermeneutics; the interpretive process of feminist pedagogy is a similar concern. The revelation of women in feminist pedagogy is not so different from their revelation in the feminist literary tradition. A paraphrase of J.S. Frye illustrates the similarity between the interpretation of experience through the text and through context in the events of the classroom:

> In recognizing women's experience as both participants in and outside of the dominant culture, a feminist poetics [read pedagogy] must not only identify the novel's [read classroom's] formal and linguistic conventions as they nearly silence women's expression, it must also assess the novel's [read classroom's] susceptibility to women's subversive expressions and the development of new conventions responsive to the experiences of women's lives and the needs of cultural change. (1986, 16)

The poetics of the novel and the pedagogy of the classroom are the intangible media by which writing and teaching are performed. A feminist hermeneutics that is central to both teaching and writing comprises these parts: understanding, interpretation, and application of texts and contexts. The interpretation of texts in feminist literary criticism is one part of a feminist hermeneutics, and the application of feminist pedagogical practice in the classroom is another. We are constantly immersed in the hermeneutical process with texts, context, each other, and ourselves.

In discussing how women are represented at the university and what this implies in political terms, I refer to Weedon.

> Modes of subjectivity, like theories of society or versions of history, are temporary fixings in the on-going process in which any absolute meaning or truth is constantly deferred. The important point is to recognize the political implications of particular ways of fixing identity and meaning. From this perspective it is clear that we are far from achieving a society in which gender, race or class are non-issues. (1987, 173)

In this ongoing process, feminist pedagogy struggles against the reality that patriarchy as a social construction is located both inside and outside of each person; similarly, the feminist teacher is located in many places at once. She finds herself within a set of patriarchal practices and also outside of the practices as critic. Even if there were a clear understanding of what that influence would mean at all times and places, we cannot act completely outside a system which is constructed not only in our external reality, but inside us as well.

Feminist teachers resist the way in which the texts and contexts of the university construct meanings and positions for us as readers. According to Minnich, "the differences between male and female as politically and socially defined have been so important to the maintenance of the prevailing order that they have been proclaimed 'nonpolitical' (meaning not open to negotiation), or 'nonacademic' (not open to discussion), and 'natural' (not open to change)" (1983, 326). Feminist reading is inherently critical when it asks what and whose purposes are served by this construction of meaning. What is surprising is that, even though conditions of knowledge production at the university are often contrary to how women see the world, "women still continue to become woman" and insist that there is a difference in how their subjectivity is experienced (de Lauretis 1984, 186).

I have shown some of the shifting, duplicitous terms of that contradiction; I have not attempted to reconcile them. I have tried to illustrate that the female subject at the university is not found in a privileged nearness to nature and the body, or in essential female consciousness; nor is femaleness based on its contradiction of the masculinist tradition. The female subject is constituted by her historical experiences, self-reflection, and by her political practice in relation with social realities (ibid.).

The impetus for the construction of a feminist pedagogy, which includes the reciprocity of teaching and learning, is more than an attempt to find a testing ground for the fit between the classroom event and one's own experience, or for reshaping one's experience to merge with available patterns and a new orthodoxy of teaching; rather, the impetus for this pedagogy is a way of reassessing experience toward the possible formation of new patterns of knowledge (J.S. Frye 1986). Knowledge becomes a process or event in which learning happens along the way. The influence of institutional practices which are beyond the control of the well-intentioned educator, however, make the process of education for social change more difficult than we often realize. Knowledge as a process is pitted against knowledge as an over-wrapped package. Methodology modelled on the systematic analysis of scientific studies has infused the approach to disciplinary studies such as English. What is traditionally defined as scholarship has become a misguided activity that excludes discovery of the discourse, but includes study of a topic as if it were a "cipher to be decoded" (Barzun 1984, 101).

Just as women's mistreatment in some research studies is often the result of "bad science," many problems in education could be similarly labelled "bad teaching." As in most fields, both scientific research and the process of education have some practices that are more exemplary than others. Much fine teaching is already being done by women and men who recognize that teaching depends to a large extent on the interrelationship between gender, power, and knowledge in the classroom. The feminist project of social change in the academy occurs slowly as it parallels the change of human consciousness and action. "Feminism is a 'gestalt' or world view, not a laundry list of 'women's issues'" (Bunch 1983, 250). Neither does it confuse an excellent way with excellence itself (ibid.).

In spite of the difficulty of the task, changes have already begun, sometimes in ad hoc classes among interested women and men, given by teachers who are uncredited and unpaid for their teaching, to students who similarly receive no credit. Feminist teaching takes place across disciplines, formally and informally, in the development of feminist institutional practices and theories. The feminist intent of social change is a slow process that takes place daily in classrooms as people support each other in the subversive activity known as feminist pedagogy. Women articulate the political, self-reflective, and historical practices of their lives; their experiences are recognized and recreated in the writing and interpersonal activities they share with other women. Women affirm the right to use both the heart *and* head in learning, and to speak, argue, and debate in classes without translation. In classes of feminist theory and in workshops, women share their views, read each other's literature, and hear that we are not isolated.

When we were doing our thesis work, a student friend of mine and I took odd comfort from the realization that the writing difficulties we were having were not caused only by our personal limitations, but that the work really was difficult. In the same milieu and given the same reaction to public expression of a feminist voice, I think that feminist pedagogy is also difficult. The difficulty increases when a person does not feel she has the right to speak, write, or teach as she wishes. I think it takes courage to address these fears—to imagine and practice as students and teachers in their own voices—without translation.

While my intent has been to read and describe the terrain wherein these acts of courage take place, others have written more specifically of the various principles and characteristics of feminist pedagogy. These descriptions include the subtleties of class discussions, the detection of the learning moments and seconds, the resistance and class dynamics that can only be solved, if at all, by making the resistance problematic. If we have some understanding of the hostility of the university context for feminist practice, we can appreciate how, even though the work is difficult, many are already involved and have written about how they make feminist pedagogy possible.

What hope is there for the continued application of this feminist process?

Feminist efforts to practice alternative forms of scholarship and pedagogy within the institution are not so much the makings of a program of reform but of revolution (Thibault 1987, 171). In that women's acceptance into academe has thus far been predicated on men's terms, a reform-oriented strategy based on masculinist notions of progress, equality, and amelioration would repeat the history of women's oppression. Within institutions, feminist change is not usually a smooth transition; in spite of its reasonableness, it will not necessarily be pleasing or polite, but disruptive, chaotic, risk-taking, and discordant. We should recall that a silencing technique effectively used on women in the past, is to call their discord "hysteria."

Herbert Marcuse suggests that revolutionary activity happens when marginalized people refuse to play the game and that this refusal may be what marks the beginning of the end of a period (1964, 257). His own philosophy of critical theory ends in negativity and possesses no hope for a better future. But while the first line of defence in the midst of emotional turmoil is always denial, many people engaged in the feminist project for social change have already moved beyond such denial. Marcuse, although personally despairing, concludes that if there is a chance for success, it is with students and with those who, "without hope, have given and give their life to the Great Refusal" (ibid.). In feminist pedagogy, the hope is in the speaking as well as in the acting.

I have looked at the work performed by the coded information at the university concerning its tacit support for its tradition. In feminist education, we can examine the messages transmitted through the masculinist codes and know that our examination, in itself, helps to transform the codes, even as it transforms us as we do the examining.

This book captures a short moment in the reading I have done, reading which began long before I started writing and which continues after the end of these pages. There is no closure in the traditional sense because the reading is not over yet, and now you have joined it too. This study illustrates one small way in which the tradition of thesis writing changed. Your reading and my writing transform the codes at the same time that we are constituted by their representation. As we interact with the university tradition, we are the subjects of our own reading.

In its representation of feminist pedagogy, we see that knowledge is not found in the arrival at a specific destination, but as in the words of R.S. Peters, "to be educated is not to have arrived; it is to travel with a different view" (1969, 123). In the interpretation of women's lives in the university context, we read of the importance of being on the way.

Selected Bibliography

Adamson, N., L. Briskin, and M. McPhail. 1988. *Feminist Organizing for Change: The Contemporary Women's Movement in Canada.* Toronto: Oxford University Press.

Aiken, S. H., ed. 1988. *Changing Our Minds: Feminist Transformation of Knowledge.* Albany: State University of New York.

Alcoff, L. 1988. "Cultural Feminism Versus Poststructuralism: The Identity Crisis in Feminist Theory" in E. Minnich, J. O'Barr, and R. Rosenfeld, eds., *Reconstructing the Academy: Women's Education and Women's Studies.* Chicago: University of Chicago Press.

Alexander, A. 1991. "Critical Social Theory: A Perspective for Critiquing Professionalization in Adult Education." *The Canadian Journal for the Study of Adult Education* 5:120-32.

Andersen, M. L. 1988. "Changing the Curriculum in Higher Education" in E. Minnich, J. O'Barr, and R. Rosenfeld, eds., *Reconstructing the Academy: Women's Education and Women's Studies.* Chicago: University of Chicago Press.

Atwood, M. 1982. *Second Words: Selected Critical Prose.* Toronto: Anansi.

Barry, K. 1991. "Deconstructing Deconstructionism (Or, Whatever Happened to Feminist Studies?)." *Ms* 1(4):83-85.

Bartby, S. L. 1979. "Toward a Phenomenology of Feminist Consciousness" in S. Bishop and M. Weinzweig, eds., *Philosophy and Women*. Belmont, CA: Wadsworth Publishing.

Barthes, R. 1972. "The Death of the Author" in S. Sears and G. W. Lord, eds., *The Discontinuous Universe: Selected Writings in Contemporary Consciousness*. New York: Basic Books.

Barzun, J. 1984. "Scholarship Versus Culture." *The Atlantic Monthly* November:93-104.

Baym, N. 1987. "The Madwoman and Her Languages: Why I Don't Do Feminist Literary Theory" in S. Benstock, ed., *Feminist Issues in Literary Analysis*. Bloomington: Indiana University Press.

Belenky, M. F., B.M. Clinchy, N.R. Goldberger, and J.M. Tarule. 1986. *Women's Ways of Knowing: The Development of Self, Voice and Mind*. New York: Basic Books.

Berger, J. 1972. *Ways of Seeing*. London: British Broadcasting Corporation and Penguin Books.

Bernikow, L. 1974. "Introduction" in L. Bernikow, ed., *The World Split Open: Four Centuries of Women Poets in England and America*. New York: Vintage.

Bezucha, R. 1985. "Feminist Pedagogy as a Subversive Activity" in M. Culley and C. Portuges, eds., *Gendered Subjects: The Dynamics of Feminist Teaching*. Boston: Routledge and Kegan Paul.

Birch, D. 1989. *Language, Literature and Critical Practice: Ways of Analysing Text*. London: Routledge.

Briskin, L. 1990. "Feminist Pedagogy" in R. Coulter, Chair, *Feminist Teaching*. Conference conducted at the meeting of the Canadian Women's Studies Association, Victoria, B.C. (May).

———. 1992. *Feminist Pedagogy: Teaching and Learning Liberation, Feminist Perspective Féministes no.19*. Ottawa: Canadian Research Institute for the Advancement of Women.

Brookes, A. 1992. *Feminist Pedagogy: An Autobiographical Approach.*

Halifax: Fernwood.

Bunch, C. 1983. "Not by Degress: Feminist Theory and Education" in C. Bunch and S. Pollack, eds., *Learning our Way: Essays in Feminist Education*. Trumansburg, NY: The Crossing Press.

Cameron, A. 1989. "Classism, Racism, and Academic Elitism Run Headlong into Low-Rent Criticism" in A. Miles and G. Finn, eds., *Feminism in Canada*. Montreal: Black Rose Books.

CAUT (Canadian Association of University Teachers). 1988. *Preamble of a Proposal for a Policy Statement on Tenure and Promotion*. Saskatoon: University of Saskatchewan.

Cocks, J. 1985. "Suspicious Pleasures: On Teaching Feminist Theory" in M. Culley and C. Portuges, eds., *Gendered Subjects*. Oxon: Routledge and Kegan Paul.

———. 1990. *The Oppositional Imagination: Feminism, Critique and Political Theory*. London: Routledge.

Collard, S. 1990. "Skirting the Issue? A Response to Angela Miles." *The Canadian Journal for the Study of Adult Education* 4(1):45-52.

Culler, J. 1982. *On Deconstruction: Theory and Criticism after Structuralism*. Ithaca, NY: University of Oklahoma Press.

———. 1988. *Framing the Sign: Criticism and its Institutions*. Norman: University of Oklahoma Press.

Culley, M. 1985. "Anger and Authority in the Introductory Women's Studies Classroom" in M. Culley and C. Portuges, eds., *Gendered Subjects: The Dynamics of Feminist Teaching*. Boston: Routledge and Kegan Paul.

Currie, D. 1989. "At the Crossraods: Feminism or Science?" in D. H. Currie, ed., *From the Margins to the Centre: Essays in Women's Studies Research*. Saskatoon: University of Saskatchewan, Women's Studies Research Unit.

Daurio, B. 1991. "Order and Imagination." (Interview with Nicole Brossard) *Books in Canada* XX(2):19-21.

de Lauretis, T. 1984. *Alice Doesn't: Feminism, Semiotics, Cinema.* Bloomington: Indiana University Press.

Donovan, J. 1987. "Toward a Women's Poetics" in S. Benstock, ed., *Feminist Issues in Literary Scholarship.* Bloomington: Indiana University Press.

Donovan, J., ed. 1989. *Feminist Literary Criticism: Explorations in Theory.* Lexington: University Press of Kentucky.

Draine, B. 1989. "Refusing the Wisdom of Solomon: Some Recent Feminist Literary Theory." *Signs: Journal of Women in Culture and Society* 15(1):144-70.

Dubois, E. C., G.P. Kelly, E.L. Kennedy, C.W. Korsmeyer, and L.S. Robinson. 1985. *Feminist Scholarship: Kindling the Groves of Academe.* Urbana: University of Illinois Press.

Eagleton, T. 1983. *Literary Theory: An Introduction.* Minneapolis: University of Minnesota Press.

Eichler, M. 1988. *Nonsexist Research Methods: A Practical Guide.* Boston: Allen and Unwin.

Ellsworth, E. 1989. "Why Doesn't this Feel Empowering? Working through the Repressive Myths of Critical Pedagogy." *Harvard Educational Review* 59(3):297-324.

Fetterley, J. 1978. *The Resisting Reader: A Feminist Approach to American Fiction.* Bloomington: Indiana University Press.

Flax, J. 1990. "Postmodernism and Gender Relations in Feminist Theory" in L. J. Nicholson, ed., *Feminism/Postmodernism.* New York: Routledge.

Flynn, E. A., and P.P. Schweickart, eds. 1986. *Gender and Reading: Essays on Readers, Texts, and Contexts.* Baltimore: The Johns Hopkins University Press.

Foucault, M. 1980. *Power/Knowledge: Selected Interviews and Other Writings: 1972-1977* C. Gordon, L. Marshall, J. Mepham, and K. Soper, trans. New York: Pantheon.

Fraser, N., and L.J. Nicholson. 1990. "Social Criticism without Philosophy" in L. J. Nicholson, ed., *Feminism/Postmodernism.* New York: Routledge.

Freire, P. 1974. *Pedagogy of the Oppressed.* M. Bergman Ramos, trans. New York: Seabury Press.

Freyerabend, P. 1976. *Against Method.* New York: Humanities Press.

Friedman, M. 1987. "Beyond Caring: The De-moralization of Gender" in M. Hanen and K. Nielsen, eds., *Science, Morality and Feminist Theory.* Calgary: University of Calgary Press.

Frye, J. S. 1986. *Living Stories, Telling Lives.* Ann Arbor: University of Michigan Press.

Frye, N. 1957. *Anatomy of Criticism: Four Essays.* New York: Atheneum.
———. 1975. "Expanding Eyes." *Critical Inquiry* 11:201-02.

Garry, A., and M. Pearsall, eds. 1989. *Women, Knowledge, and Reality: Explorations in Feminist Philosophy.* Boston: Unwin Hyman.

Gaskell, J., and A. McLaren, eds. 1987. *Women and Education: A Canadian Perspective.* Calgary: Detselig Enterprises.

Gaskell, J., A. McLaren, and M. Novogrodsky. 1989. *Claiming an Education: Feminist and Canadian Schools.* Toronto: Our Schools/ Our Selves Monograph Series 3.

Gearhart, S. M. 1983. "If the Mortoboard Fits . . ." in C. Bunch and S. Pollock, eds., *Learning our Way: Essays in Feminist Education.* Trumansburg, NY: The Crossing Press.

Gilligan, C. 1982. *In a Different Voice.* Cambridge, MA: Harvard University Press.

Giroux, H. 1988. "Postmodernism and the Discourse of Educational Criticism." *Journal of Education* 170(3):5-30.

Glaspell, S. 1916. "A Jury of her Peers" in F. J. O'Brien, ed., *The Best American Short Stories.* Boston: Houghton Mifflin.

Grant, G. 1969. "The University Curriculum." *Technology and Empire*. Toronto: House of Anansi.

Hammer, B. 1983. "Creative Teaching Spaces: Home Movies" in C. Bunch and S. Pollack, eds., *Learning our Way: Essays in Feminist Education*. Trumansburg, NY: The Crossing Press.

Harding, S., ed. 1987a. *Feminism and Methodology*. Bloomington: Indiana University Press.

Harding, S. 1987b. "Ascetic Intellectual Opportunities: Reply to Alison Wylie" in M. Hanen and K. Nielsen, eds., *Science, Morality and Feminist Theory*. Calgary: University of Calgary Press.

Harding, S., and M.B. Hintikka, eds. 1983. *Discovering Reality: Feminist Perspectives on Epistemology, Metaphysics, Methodology and Philosophy of Science*. Boston: Reidel.

Hartsock, N. 1990. "Foucault on Power: A Theory of Women?" in L. J. Nicholson, ed., *Feminism/Postmodernism*. New York: Routledge.

Hawkesworth, M. E. 1989. "Knowers, Knowing, Known: Feminist Theory and Claims of Truth." *Signs* 14(3):533-57.

Hayes, E. 1993. "Current Perspectives on Teaching Adults." *Adult Education Quarterly* 43(3):173-86.

Heald, S. 1989. "The Madwoman out of the Attic: Feminist Teaching in the Margins." *Resources for Feminist Research* 18(4):22-26.

———. 1991. "Pianos to Pedagogy: Pursuing the Educational Subject" in H. Bannerji, L. Carty, K. Dehli, S. Heald, and K. McKenna, eds., *Unsettling Relations: The University as a Site of Feminist Struggles*. Toronto: Women's Press.

Hekman, S. 1992. *Gender and Knowledge: Elements of a Postmodern Feminism*. Boston: Northeastern University Press.

Hillyer Davis, B. 1985. "Teaching the Feminist Minority" in M. Culley and C. Portuges, eds., *Gendered Subjects: The Dynamics of Feminist Teaching*. Boston: Routledge and Kegan Paul.

Hoffman, N. J. 1985. "Breaking Silences: Life in the Feminist Classroom" in M. Culley and C. Portuges, eds., *Gendered Subjects: The Dynamics of Feminist Teaching*. Boston: Routledge and Kegan Paul.

Howe, F. 1983. "Feminist Scholarship: The Extent of the Revolution" in C. Bunch and S. Pollack, eds., *Learning our Way: Essays in Feminist Education*. Trumansburg, NY: The Crossing Press.

Hughes, M., and M. Kennedy. 1983. "Breaking Out—Women in Adult Education." *Women's Studies International Forum* 6(3):261-70.

Hutcheon, L. 1989. *The Politics of Postmodernism*. London: Routledge.

Innis Dagg, A. 1992. "Feminism Reviled: Academic Non-freedom at Canadian Universities." *Canadian Women Studies* 12(3):89-92.

Jacobus, M. 1986. *Reading Woman: Essays in Feminist Criticism*. New York: Columbia University Press.

Jagger, A. 1983. *Feminist Politics and Human Nature*. Sussex, England: The Harvard Press.

Jean, M. 1984. "Creating and Communicating Knowledge from a Feminist Perspective: The Risks and Challenges for Women" in *Knowledge Reconsidered: A Feminist Overview*. Ottawa: Proceedings from the Canadian Research Institute for the Advancement of Women, Vancouver, 1983.

Johnson, B. 1987. *A World of Difference*. London: Johns Hopkins University Press.

Kennard, J. E. 1981. "Convention Coverage or How to Read Your Own Text." *New Literary History* 13(1):69-88.

Kingdom, E. 1987. "Feminism and Philosophy." *Resources for Feminist Research* 16(3):8-9.

Klein, R. D., and D.L. Steinberg, eds. 1989. *Radical Voices: A Decade of Feminist Resistance from "Women's Studies International Forum."* New York: Pergamon Press.

Kohlberg, J. 1973. "Continuities and Discontinuities in Childhood and

Adult Moral Development Revisited" in *Collected Papers on Moral Development and Moral Education.* Boston: Moral Education Research Foundation, Harvard University.

Kolodny, A. 1975. *The Lay of the Land: Metaphor as Experience in American Life and Letters.* Chapel Hill: University of North Carolina Press.

———. 1980. "A Map for Rereading: Or, Gender and the Interpretation of Literary Texts." *New Literary History* 11(3):451-67.

Krall, F.R. 1988. "From the Inside Out—Personal History as Educational Research." *Educational Theory* 38(4):467-79.

Kuhn, T. S., 1970. *The Structure of Scientific Revolutions* (2). Chicago: University of Chicago Press.

Kuykendall, E. 1981. "Feminist Linguistics in Philosophy" in M. Vetterling-Braggin, ed., *Sexist Language: A Modern Philosophical Analysis.* Littlefield: Adams and Company.

Lacan, J. 1977. *Ecrits: A Selection.* A. Sheridan, trans. New York: W. W. Norton and Company.

LaFontaine, P. W. 1981. *Non-Sexist Education: Toward the Emergence of an Alternative Curriculum Paradigm for Women's Studies Programs.* Unpublished doctoral dissertation, Ohio State Universtiy.

Langland, E., and W. Gove, eds. 1983. *A Feminist Perspective in the Academy: The Difference it Makes.* Chicago: University of Chicago Press.

Lather, P. 1986. "Issues of Validity in Openly Ideological Research: Between a Rock and a Soft Place." *Interchange* 17(4):63-84.

———. 1989. "Postmodernism and Politics of Enlightenment." *Educational Foundations* 3(3):7-28.

Leach, B. 1988. "Teacher Education and Reform: What's Sex Got To Do With It?" *Educational Foundations* 2(2):4-14.

Leach, B., and B. Davies. 1990. "Crossing the Boundaries: Educational

Thought and Gender Equity." *Educational Theory* 40(3):321-32.

Lebowitz, A. 1983. "Hindsight is 20/20: The Development, Achievements and Dilemmas of Feminist Literary Criticism." in *Knowledge Reconsidered: A Feminist Overview*. Ottawa: Proceedings from the Canadian Research Institute for the Advancement of Women, Vancouver, 1983.

le Doeuff, M. 1977 "Women and Philosophy." *Radical Philosophy* 17, Summer.

Lentricchia, F. 1990. "In Place of an Afterword—Someone Reading" in F. Lentricchia and T. McLaughlin, eds., *Critical Terms for Literary Study*. Chicago: University of Chicago Press.

Lewis, M. 1990. "Interrupting Patriarchy: Politics, Resistance, and Transformation in the Feminist Classroom." *Harvard Educational Review* 60(4):467-88.

Lewis, M., and R.I. Simon. 1986. "Discourse Not Intended for Her: Teaching and Learning within Patriarchy." *Harvard Educational Review* 56:457-72.

Lloyd, G. 1984. *The Man of Reason: "Male" and "Female" in Western Philosophy*. Minneapolis: University of Minnesota Press.

Lobban, G. 1977. "Sexist Bias in Reading Schemes" in M. Hoyles, ed., *The Politics of Literacy*. London: Readers' and Writers' Publishing Co-op.

Lugones, M. C., and E.V. Spelman. 1986. "Have We Got a Theory for You! Feminist Theory, Cultural Imperialism and the Demand for 'The Women's Voice'" in M. Pearsall, ed., *Women and Values: Readings in Recent Feminist Philosophy*. Belmont, CA: Wadsworth.

MacCormack, T. 1983. "The Political Culture and the Press of Canada." *Canadian Journal of Political Science* 26(3):451-72.

Maher, F. 1985. "Classroom Pedagogy and the New Scholarship on Women" in M. Culley and C. Portuges, eds., *Gendered Subjects: The Dynamics of Feminist Teaching*. Boston: Routledge and Kegan Paul.

Malson, M. R., J.F. O'Barr, S. Westphal-Wihl, and M. Wyer, eds. 1989. *Feminist Theory in Practice and Process*. Chicago: University of Chicago.

Marcuse, H. 1964. *One-Dimensional Man: Studies in the Ideology of Advanced Industrial Society*. Boston: Beacon Press.

Martindale, K. 1987. "On the Ethics of 'Voice' in Feminist Literary Criticism." *Resources for Feminist Research* 16(3):6-19.

McLaren, A. T. 1985. *Ambitions and Realizations: Women in Adult Education*. London: Peter Owen.

Meese, E. 1986. *Crossing the Double-Cross: The Practice of Feminist Criticism*. Chapel Hill: University of North Carolina Press.

Merriam, S., ed. 1983. *Themes of Adulthood Through Literature*. New York: Teachers' College Press.

Mickelson, R. A. 1989. "Why Does Jane Read and Write So Well? The Anomoly of Women's Achievement." *Sociology of Education* 62:47-63.

Miles, A. 1989. "Women's Challenge to Adult Education." *The Canadian Journal for the Study of Adult Eucation* 3(1):1-18.

Miles, A., and G. Finn, eds. 1982. *Feminism in Canada: From Pressure to Politics*. Montreal: Black Rose Books.

———. 1989. *Feminism: From Pressure to Politics*. Montreal: Black Rose Books.

Miller, N. 1991. *Getting Personal: Feminist Occasions and Other Autobiographical Acts*. New York: Routledge.

Minnich, E. K. 1983. "Friends and Critics: The Feminist Academy" in C. Bunch and S. Pollack, eds., *Learning our Way: Essays in Feminist Education*. Trumansburg, NY: The Crossing Press.

Moi, T. 1985. *Sexual/Textual Politics: Feminist Literary Theory*. London: Methuen.

Nemiroff, G. H. 1989. "Beyond 'Talking Heads:' Towards an Empowering Pedagogy of Women's Studies." *Atlantis* 15(1):1-16.

Nicholson, L. J., ed. 1990. *Feminism/Postmodernism.* New York: Routledge.

Noddings, N. 1984. *Caring: A Feminine Approach to Ethics and Moral Education.* Berkeley: University of California Press.

———. 1985. "In Search of the Feminine." *Philosophy of Education 1985.* Proceedings of the forty-fourth annual meeting of the Philosophy of Education Society, Normal, IL.

———. 1986. "Fidelity in Teaching, Teacher Education, and Research for Teaching." *Harvard Educational Review* 56(4):496-510.

———. 1989. *Developing Models of Caring in the Professions.* Paper presented at the meeting of the Annual Educational Research Association, San Fransisco, CA (March).

Oakley, A. 1981. "Interviewing Women: A Contradiction in Terms" in H. Roberts, ed., *Doing Feminist Research.* London: Routledge and Kegan Paul.

Palmer, R. E. 1969. *Hermeneutics: Interpretation Theory in Schleiermacher, Dilthey, Heidegger, and Gadamer.* Evanston: Northwestern University Press.

Pateman, C., and E. Gross, eds. 1986. *Feminist Challenges: Social and Political Theory.* Boston: Northeastern University Press.

Pope, D. 1989. "Notes Toward a Supreme Fiction: The Work of Feminist Criticism" in J. F. O'Barr, ed., *Women and a New Academy: Gender and Cultural Contexts.* Madison: University of Wisconsin Press.

Powe, B. W. 1985. *A Climate Charged.* Oakville: Mosaic Press.

Price, L. S. 1988. *In Women's Interests: Feminist Activism and Institutional Change.* Vancouver: Women's Research Centre.

Probyn, E. 1990. "Travels in the Postmodern: Making Sense of the Local" in L. J. Nicholson, ed., *Feminism/Postmodernism.* New York:

Routledge.

Raymond, J. G. 1985. "Women's Studies: A Knowledge of One's Own" in M. Culley and C. Portuges, eds., *Gendered Subjects: The Dynamics of Feminist Teaching*. Boston: Routledge and Kegan Paul.

Rich, A. 1979. *On Lies, Secrets, and Silence: Selected Prose 1966-1978*. New York: W. W. Norton and Company.

Ricoeur, P. 1981. "The Model of the Text: Meaningful Action Considered as a Text" in J.B. Thompson, ed., *Paul Ricoeur: Hermeneutics and the Human Sciences: Essays on Language, Action and Interpretation*. J.B. Thompson, trans. Cambridge: Cambridge University Press.

Robinson, L.S. 1985. "Treason Our Text: Feminist Challenges to the Literary Canon" in E. Showalter, ed., *The New Feminist Criticism: Essays on Women, Literature, and Theory*. New York: Pantheon.

Rockhill, K. 1989. "e-MAN-ci-patory Literacy: An Essay Review of Literacy: Reading the Word and the World." *Canadian Women's Studies* 9 (3and4):113-15.

Rooke, P. 1989. "Re-ordering our Partiality: Reflections on Careerism and Feminist Commitment in Academia." *The Journal of Educational Thought* 23:106-29.

Russell, M. 1985. "Black-eyed Blues Connections: Teaching Black Women" in M. Culley and C. Portuges, eds., *Gendered Subjects: The Dynamics of Feminist Teaching*. Boston: Routledge and Kegan Paul.

Sandilands, K. 1990. *Correlations and Consciousness-Raising: Toward an Understanding of Feminism, Method, and Liberatory Strategy*. Presented at a conference conducted at the meeting of the Canadian Sociology and Anthropology Associations, Victoria, B.C. (June).

Schaef, A. W. 1982. *Women's Reality: An Emerging Female System in the White Male Society*. Minneapolis: Winston Press.

Schaef, A. W., and D. Fassel. 1988. *The Addictive Organization*. San Francisco: Harper and Row.

Schniedewind, N., and E. Davidson. 1983. *Open Minds to Equality: A*

Sourcebook of Promoting Race, Sex, and Age Equality. Englewood Cliffs: Prentice Hall.

Schuster, M., and S. VanDyne. 1985. *Women's Place in the Academy: Transforming the Liberal Arts Curriculum*. Totawa, NJ: Rowan and Allenheld.

Schweickart, P.P. 1986. "Reading Ourselves: Toward a Feminist Theory of Reading" in E. A. Flynn and P. P. Schweickart, eds., *Gender and Reading: Essays on Readers, Texts, and Contexts*. London: Johns Hopkins University Press.

Sherwin, S. 1984. "From Feminism to a New Conception of Ethics." in *Knowledge Reconsidered: A Feminist Overview*. Ottawa: Proceedings from the Canadian Research Institute for the Advancement of Women, Vancouver, 1983.

———. 1987. "A Feminist Approach to Ethics." *Resources for Feminist Research* 16(3):25-28.

Shogan, D. 1987. "The Philosophical Question in Feminism." *Resources for Feminist Research* 16(3):10-11.

Showalter, E. 1987. "Women's Time, Women's Space: Writing the History of Feminist Criticism" in S. Benstock, ed., *Feminist Issues in Literary Scholarship*. Bloomington: Indiana University Press.

Showalter, E., ed. 1985. *The New Feminist Criticism: Essays on Women, Literature, and Theory*. New York: Pantheon Books.

Smith, D. E. 1974. "The Social Construction of Documentary Reality." *Sociological Inquiry* 44:258-67.

———. 1984. "The Renaissance of Women." in *Knowledge Reconsidered: A Feminist Overview*. Ottawa: Proceedings from the Canadian Research Institute for the Advancement of Women, Vancouver, 1983.

———. 1987a. "An Analysis of Ideological Structures and How Women are Excluded: Consideration for Academic Women" in J. Gaskell and A. McLaren, eds., *Women and Education: A Canadian Perspective*. Calgary: Detselig Enterprises.

———. 1987b. *The Everyday World as Problematic: A Feminist Sociology*. Toronto: University of Toronto Press.

Smith, G. A. 1991. "Affirmative Action in Faculty Hiring: A Reply to J. E. Miller." *Vox* January:1-3.

Snoek, D. 1985. "A Male Feminist in a Women's College Classroom" in M. Culley and C. Portuges, eds., *Gendered Subjects: The Dynamics of Feminist Teaching*. Boston: Routledge and Kegan Paul.

Spelman, E. V. 1988. *Inessential Woman: Problems of Exclusion in Feminist Thought*. Boston: Beacon Press.

Spender, D. 1986. *Mothers of the Novel: 100 Good Women Writers before Jane Austen*. London: Pandora Press.

Spender, D., ed. 1981. *Men's Studies Modified: The Impact of Feminism on the Academic Disciplines*. Toronto: Pergamon Press.

Spivak, G.C. 1988. "Can the Subaltern Speak?" in C. Nelson and L. Grossberg, eds., *Marxism and the Interpretation of Culture*. Urbana: University of Illinois Press.

———. 1990. "Question on Multi-Culturalism" in S. Harasym, ed., *The Post-Colonial Critic: Interviews, Strategies, Dialogues*. New York: Routledge.

Stanley, L., and S. Wise. 1983. *Breaking Out: Feminist Consciousness and Feminist Research*. London: Routledge and Kegan Paul.

Storrie, K. 1989. "The Everyday World as Problematic: A Bridge Between the Academy and the Universtiy" in D. H. Currie, ed., *From the Margins to the Centre: Essays in Women's Studies Research*. Saskatoon: University of Saskatchewan, Women's Studies Research Unit.

Sydie, R. 1989. "Scientific Research and Feminist Critiques: Co-operation and Competition as Contested Terrain" in D. H. Currie, ed., *From the Margins to the Centre: Essays in Women's Studies Research*. Saskatoon: University of Saskatchewan, Women's Studies Research Unit.

Thibault, G. M. 1987. *The Dissenting Feminist Academy: A History of*

Barriers to Feminist Scholarship. New York: Peter Lang.

Tomm, W., ed. 1989. *The Effects of Feminist Approaches on Research Methodologies*. Waterloo: Wilfred Laurier University Press.

Walsh, A. 1986. "A Theory Narrative in Five Movements: The Maps are Drawn by a Living Choir: Contexts for the Practice of a Feminist Metatheory of Literary History." *Interchange* 17(1):1-22.

Warren, C. 1987. "Feminist Discourse and the Research Enterprise: Implications for Adult Education." *Canadian Journal for the Study of Adult Education* 1(2):23-42.

Weedon, C. 1987. *Feminist Practice and Poststructuralist Theory*. New York: Basil Blackwell.

Weiler, K. 1991. "Freire and a Feminist Pedagogy of Difference." *Harvard Educational Review* 61(4):449-74.

Weisman, K. L., and N.P. Birkby. 1983. "The Women's School of Planning and Architecture" in C. Bunch and S. Pollack, eds., *Learning our Way: Essays in Feminist Education*. Trumansburg, NY: The Crossing Press.

White, B. M. 1986. "Training Women Leaders: A Model Program" in P. A. Farrant, ed., *Strategies and Attitudes—Women in Education Administration—A Book of Readings*. Washington, DC: National Association for Women Deans, Administrators, and Counselors.

Wilcox, H., and A. Thompson, eds. 1989. *Teaching Women: Feminism and English Studies*. Manchester: Manchester University Press.

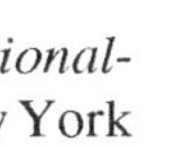

Wilshire, B. 1990. *The Moral Collapse of the University: Professionalism, Purity, and Alienation*. New York: State University of New York Press.

Woolf, V. 1966. *Three Guineas*. New York: Harcourt Brace.

———. 1982. *A Room of One's Own*. London: Granada.

Wylie, A. 1987. "The Philosophy of Ambivalence: Sandra Harding on 'The Science Question in Feminism'" in M. Hanen and K. Nielsen, eds., *Science, Morality and Feminist Theory*. Calgary: University of Calgary Press.

Wylie. A., and K. O'Kruhlik. 1987. "Philosophical Feminism: Challenges to Science." *Resources for Feminist Research* 16(3):12-15.

Young, I. M. 1990. "The Ideal of Community and the Politics of Difference" in L. J. Nicholson, ed., *Feminism/Postmodernism*. New York: Routledge.

Zacharakis-Jutz, J. 1988. "Post-Freirean Adult Education: A Question of Empowerment and Power." *Adult Education Quarterly* 39(1):41-47.

Related Titles from Fernwood Publishing

BECOMING AN ALLY
Breaking the Cycle of Oppression
Anne Bishop
This book is a dialogue—by a white, lesbian feminist who co-leads with a Black colleague a workshop on racism—about the answers to questions on the nature of oppression: where does it come from, has it always been with us, what can we do to change it, what does individual healing have to do with struggles for social justice, why do members of the same oppressed group fight each other, why do some who experience oppression develop a life-long commitment to fighting oppression, while others turn around and become oppressors themselves?
137pp Paper ISBN 1 895686 39 3 $13.95

ECOFEMINISM
Maria Mies and Vandana Shiva
Mies and Shiva write a powerful critique of the ideas of the Enlightenment, which measured civilization in terms of the domination of Nature. They argue that feminism should see linkages between patriarchal oppression and the destruction of Nature in the name of profit and progress. Through examining issues such as the growth of new reproductive technologies, "development," indigenous knowledge, globalization, the concepts of freedom and self-determination, the authors provide a vision of a different value system.
288pp Paper ISBN 1 895686 28 8 $25.95

FEMINISM AND THE POLITICS OF DIFFERENCE
Sneja Gunew and Anna Yeatman eds.
Increasingly "Western" feminism is being challenged to confront the multiple characters of domination and exploitation, usually conceived of as gender, class, race, and ethnicity. This innovative and timely collection reveals exciting contemporary theorising; raising and exploring the problems posed by identity politics and the possibilities for non-exclusive cultural and gendered positions.
254pp Paper ISBN 1 895686 27 X $19.95

. . . continued

FEMINIST PEDAGOGY
An Autobiographical Approach
Anne-Louise Brookes
"To weave as you have woven is to concretize an abstract concept. . . . In doing this you have provided a very important suspension bridge to that eventual validation of blending Self with Knowledge. Traversing that bridge will result in some potential followers wobbling and some falling, but those who can reach the other side will be allies in the greater battle of education for Human's sake rather than for Academe's sake; more specifically, to acknowledge the requirement of including personal life spaces in the thought processes involved in taking a body of knowledge as one's own" (Lisa deLeon, author of *Writers of Newfoundland and Labrador*).
195pp Paper ISBN 1 895686 00 8 $15.95

LIMITED EDITION
Voices of Women, Voices of Feminsim
Geraldine Finn ed.
This book is an introductory text and reader for use in Women's Studies. Feminist activists, teachers, students of Women's Studies, and women in the paid and unpaid labour force speak about their own experiences of feminism and the difference it has made in their public and private lives.
399pp Paper ISBN 1 895686 13 X $26.95

MARKETING PLACE
Cultural Politics, Regionalism and Reading
Ursula S. Kelly
This book incorporates aspects of feminism, political economy, literary theory, social psychology and critical educational theory to demonstrate the socio-political and cultural dimensions of reading and identity. Newfoundland readers of Newfoundland books provide a specific focus for an investigation of the intersections of region, place, culture, power and identity.
100pp Paper ISBN 1 895686 16 4 $11.95 (From the Fernwood *Basics* series)

MAID IN THE MARKET
Women's Paid Domestic Labour
Sedef Arat-Koç and Wenona Giles eds.
Chapters on domestic workers, chambermaids, daycare workers, the retail sector, the fast food industry, and home and office cleaners demonstrate that the work of reproduction in capitalist society is subordinated and devalued in the marketplace as well as at home.
160pp Paper ISBN 1 895686 35 0 $15.95

NO GOING BACK
Women as University Students
Patricia Campbell
Today, more older women are choosing to return to school. What kinds of rewards and difficulties do they encounter? What inspires them to seek a university education? What kind of support do they receive from their partners and children, from teachers and younger students? Allowing these women to tell their stories in their own voices, this book reveals their collective experience in all its complexity.
91pp Paper ISBN 1 895686 22 9 $11.95 (From the Fernwood *Basics* series)

THE POWER OF WOMAN-POSITIVE LITERACY WORK
Program-based action research
Betty-Ann Lloyd with Frances Ennis and Tannis Atkinson
Thirty women from across Canada participated in a program-based action research project that asked the question—What happens when some women in an adult literacy or basic education program do something they define as woman-positive? The different stories of their experiences are published in this and the next two books. This first book provides the background for the research, details the research process, and describes each program, its community and woman-positive activity. It contains a collaborative analysis and recommendations developed by the women directly involved.
280pp Paper ISBN 1 895686 36 9 $18.00 ($38.00 for the set of three books)

WOMEN IN LITERACY SPEAK
The power of woman-positive literacy work
Betty-Ann Lloyd with Frances Ennis and Tannis Atkinson eds.
The women involved in this program-based action research documented their experience in different ways—published material, reflective and analytical articles, interviews and journals, a policy paper, and a story suitable for use as curriculum. This book includes all of this documentation, as well as a discussion of two central issues from the exploratory phase of the research, a summary of the research process, collaborative analysis, and recommendations.
216pp Paper ISBN 895686 37 7 $15.00 ($38.00 for the set of three books)

LISTEN TO WOMEN IN LITERACY
The power of woman-positive literacy work
Tannis Atkinson with Frances Ennis and Betty-Ann Lloyd
Written and designed for use by intermediate and advanced students in adult literacy and basic education programs, this book adapts material from the two other books that describe women's experience during this research project.
88pp Paper ISBN 1 895686 38 5 $8.00 ($38.00 for the set of three books)

Basics from Fernwood Publishing

*The **Basics** present topics of current interest—many on the cutting edge of scholarship—in a short and inexpensive format that makes them ideal as supplementary texts and for general interest. New proposals for the series are welcome.*

DIVORCE AND DISENGAGEMENT
Patterns of Fatherhood Within and Beyond Marriage
Edward Kruk
This book's purpose is to better portray divorced fatherhood and to provide family practitioners and policymakers with an empirically based understanding of the impact of divorce on non-custodial fathers, and of fathers' disengagement from their children after divorce.
138pp Paper ISBN 1 895686 23 7 $11.95

ELUSIVE JUSTICE
Beyond the Marshall Inquiry
Joy Manette ed.
The essays in this volume reveal how, even in this latest inquiry, the traditions, wisdom, customs and culture of the Mi'kmaq people were almost completely ignored.
110pp Paper ISBN 1 895686 02 4 $11.95

ISSUMATUQ
Learning from the Traditional Healing Wisdom of the Canadian Inuit
Kit Minor
Kit Minor helps us to understand what and how we can learn from the traditional helping wisdom of the Canadian Inuit. Through the develpment of a *culture-specific* design the author shows us how Inuit people, in a working relationship with members of the dominant culture, can continue to define and decide on appropriate helping skills.
112pp Paper ISBN 2 896586 05 9 $11.95

MAN'S WILL TO HURT
Investigating the Causes, Supports and Varieties of His Violence
Joseph A. Kuypers
The author contends that men have a *will to hurt*—that their use and threat of pain achieves many "benefits": power, profit, pleasure, sexual legitimacy and membership in male organized society. This book identifies how men code their *will to hurt* to make it moral, and how male violence is entrenched in society and infused into concepts of masculinity and sexuality.
127pp Paper ISBN 1 895686 06 7 $11.95

NAMES, NUMBERS, AND NORTHERN POLICY
Inuit, Project Surname, and the Politics of Identity
Valerie Alia
Names are the cornerstones of cultures. They identify individuals, represent life, express and embody power. When power is unequal and people are colonized at one level or another, naming is manipulated from the outside. In the Canadian North, the most blatant example of this manipulation is the long history of interference by visitors with the ways Inuit named themselves and their land.
120pp Paper ISBN 1 895686 31 8 $11.95

STAR WARS IN CANADIAN SOCIOLOGY
Exploring the Social Construction of Knowledge
David A. Nock
Sociological theory and social analysis are not abstractions—they evolve out of social conditions. In this book David Nock situates Canadian sociological theory within the Canadian context. He looks at the theories of prominent sociologists and presents a thoroughly grounded discussion of how this unique brand of sociology has been socially constructed.
127pp Paper ISBN 1 895686 18 0 $11.95

STIFLING DEBATE
Canadian Newspapers and Nuclear Power
Michael Clow
The Canadian Nuclear Industry claims the media have treated them unfairly and a multimillion-dollar pro-nuclear advertising campaign has been publicly funded on this pretext. This study of nuclear coverage finds that it is the promoters, not the opponents, of nuclear energy that overwhelmingly dominate news coverage. The author proposes that this coverage raises the issue of whether a new genre of news writing and a new form of news organization are needed to provide a more representative picture of political life.
123pp Paper ISBN 1 895686 15 6 $11.95